R0400044618 11/03

ALL MEAT LOOKS LIKE SOUTH AMERICA

ALL MEAT LOOKS LIKE
SOUTH AMERICA

THE WORLD OF BRUCE McCALL

By Bruce McCall

Crown Publishers
New York

Other books by Bruce McCall

Zany Afternoons
Thin Ice
The Last Dream-o-Rama

Published by Crown Publishers, New York, New York.
Member of the Crown Publishing Group, a division of Random House, Inc.
www.randomhouse.com

Most of the illustrations and text in this book have appeared in the following publications:
The New Yorker, Vanity Fair, Sky, Outside, My Generation, Discover, The Observatory,
The Washington Post Magazine, Saturday Post, and *The New York Times.*

CROWN is a trademark and the Crown colophon is a registered trademark of Random House, Inc.

Printed in China

Design by Kay Schuckhart/Blond on Pond

Library of Congress Cataloging-in-Publication Data

McCall, Bruce
All Meat Looks Like South America: The World of Bruce McCall / by Bruce McCall — 1st ed.
1. American wit and humor. 2. American wit and humor, pictorial. I. Title.
PN6165M37 2003
741.5'973—dc21   20022041407

ISBN 0-609-60802-9

10 9 8 7 6 5 4 3 2 1

First Edition

INTRODUCTION

It may not impress you, but it amazes hell out of me that this book has been twenty years in the making. That's how far back I reached for the oldest piece published herein. I bet you can't tell which one it is, however, because my editor said at the outset, "Bruce, forget the topical crap. Go with the works"—he calls my stuff "works"—"that speak to the ages, that will endure long after the relevant, the timely, and you yourself are long forgotten." And so I did, thus ensuring that the final advance payment would not be forgotten.

A great many magazine art directors and editors were press-ganged into providing much of the material that made this book possible, and for their unstinting assistance—no author ever left "unstinting assistance" out of his payback paragraph—I am even deeper in their thrall. One editor, who doesn't like me anymore, refused even stinting assistance, so almost none of my work over the years for his magazine appears here.

I think readers like authors who level with them.

My agent and friend Liz Darhansoff, my editor Doug Pepper, Thaddeus Bower, Mark McCauslin, Alison Forner, and Lauren Dong at Crown, the designer Kay Schuckhart, Jim and Kathy Goodman of the James Goodman Gallery—all deserve some of the blame if this book tanks. Doug in particular, whose unyielding decision it was to use that title, will just have to live with it.

But let's not get all down at the mouth. This book is supposed to be funny—nay, silly as a proverbial goose—and allowing a defeatist attitude to seep into the Introduction would make a poor launching platform for the hilarity with which the following pages are meant to be shot through.

Bruce McCall

Cap-Ferrat, April 2003*

* I'm nowhere near Cap-Ferrat as this is written, but have always noted with jealousy and admiration the way many upscale authors like to use this otherwise harmless little convention to flaunt their sophistication and implicit wealth and plant the idea that they're having a lot better time than you are. I am a satirist, after all. You will forgive the cheap shot?

BRUCE McCALL

PART I

CHILD OF THE ZEITGEIST

ROME IS EXACTLY THE COLOR OF DOG BISCUITS.

—ANONYMOUS

Bicker one can about his inability to draw a convincing dog, his overdependence on "funny" names, his effrontery in presuming to place another dump-truck-load of hackwork between covers; that the creator of the following body of work could get anything done at all during the period represented herein is perhaps the real triumph to be celebrated in this book. The events of the tumultuous period between 1935 and 2002 "could fill 67 fat almanacs and an encyclopedia," observed Will Durant, or William Crapo Durant, at any rate one of the Durants, maybe Ariel for all we now know. But consider: the Glassboro Summit, Princess Margaret's wedding, Newfoundland's entry into Confederation, Corfam, Judy Garland's comeback, the Studebaker-Packard merger, Expo 67, the 1968 San Antonio World's Fair, ad infinitum—each of us has his or her own such list, albeit probably not as lengthy nor as comprehensive as his, for he was further distracted by events—the Belgian waffle riots of the immediate postwar period, the launch of the first naphtha-powered submarine—that never actually happened. As if these were not distraction enough for any artist or school of artists, there was all the while the shoe-store job. There were the family feuds, the bouts of catatonia, the long walks. He even did his own washing and ironing, save of course for the Utrecht years. And yet, and yet, the work kept coming and keeps coming still. Rushed, fragmented, as often wobbly of aim as it is woozy of execution, to be sure, as if he were painting with the one hand while pasting another clipping into his Dionne Quintuplets scrapbook with the other. And withal, seemingly not a trace of profundity from first page to last, only the relentless har-har-har of the born vulgarian. We would submit that less could hardly be said of any other book of its time.

THE LOST SKETCHBOOKS OF ALBERT SPEER

After Hitler's official architect, Albert Speer,
left Spandau prison in 1966, he had big plans to rebuild his
career on the other side of the Atlantic.

Sprung from Spandau prison in 1966 after 20 years with little more to his name than a 50-deutsche-mark bill and a new ankle-length leather raincoat, Albert Speer wasted no time calling in his chits among old rocketeer chums now working for NASA. If they'd help him find architectural work in the United States, he'd burn certain sensitive wartime documents. That the official architect of the Third Reich should be scrabbling to bid on this fast-food outlet or that souvenir stand in the American hinterlands may seem a colossal comedown; Speer saw it as the start of his comeback. Forbidden to practice in a Europe that refused to let bygones be bygones, he meant to glorify even the humblest of projects with his bold and monumental vision. Soon enough, he believed, as evidence of his genius spread, America too would fall for the unique architectural style that had dominated pre-war Germany.

This was not to be. Speer's compulsive reliance on the brutish mass, the soaring column, and the mile-wide avenue may have thrilled his megalomaniacal patron Adolf Hitler; applied to a Tulsa shoe store or a Bakersfield Moose lodge, these motifs clashed with the democratic vernacular and were, in some cases, counterproductive from a mercantile point of view. Again and again, his ambitious solutions were submitted, rejected, and forgotten. Trapped in the one idiom he ever knew, Speer could only be Speer. Careerwise, it was three Reichs and you're out.

Albert Speer died in 1981 without seeing a single one of his post-Spandau visions realized in windowless stone and concrete. His American sketchbooks vanished into limbo with him—until early this year, when, in a thrift shop in Munich, a sheaf of papers was found sewn into the lining of a long leather raincoat. It was Speer's long leather raincoat, of course, and those papers were Speer's lost sketches, secreted away for fear of sullying his legend with evidence of utter failure.

Here, then, the lost sketchbooks of Albert Speer: haunting images, unseen for decades, marking the final bizarre chapter of the 20th century's most controversial architectural career.

LAST CHANCE SNAKE FARM AND SOUVENIR STAND
Page, Arizona, 1969

Soaring verticals had marked many a previous Speer concept, most notably his "cathedral of ice" for the annual Nuremberg party rally in the 30s. Transplanted to the Arizona desert in the form of three identical aluminum towers, the idea might well have worked to lure tourists from miles around to the roadside stand below, evoking the awe that buckles resistance. Proprietors Ma and Pa Jeeter had been thinking more along the lines of a repaint and a new screen door; accustomed to limitless government funds, Speer took things rather further. His bid, $15.9 million over budget, was regretfully declined.

ETERNAL CAR WASH
Bakersfield, California, 1970

As with so many Speer buildings, this automated car wash seems to pin the onlooker to the ground and render mere humans—and their cars—insignificant, while virtually demanding patronage, now. Yet there are brilliant flashes: wash suds recycled to create an imposing illuminated waterfall, both a functional cue and—with its roar magnified via loudspeakers—a symbol of raw power; a multitrack pass-through handling 2,000 autos per hour; twin "eternal flames," a favorite Speer theme here used to signal an open-24-hours policy. Pompous overstatement for a mere car wash? Perhaps. The architect himself met such quibbles with icy disdain: "Next to Speer," he thundered, "even Ozymandias looks shy."

FLOYD'Z KOZY KABINZ
Panama City, Florida, 1973

Stark and almost grimly functional, Floyd's cast-concrete Kozy Kabinz allowed—indeed, ordered—guests to drive their cars directly into their cabins. But what to make of the twin guardhouses at the south entrance, superfluous if not outright overkill in most motor-court designs? Floyd took this, as well as the cabins' total lack of fenestration and a paved landscaping plan relieved only by artificial palm trees, as a hint that Speer might lack a certain feel for the tastes of the American traveler. The rejection of his proposal broke Speer's heart. Vowing to never again waste his genius on the philistine American, he had just begun sketches for a new police academy in Paraguay at the time of his death in 1981.

MEL'S MIRACLE MILE BOWL-O-RAMA
Nazareth, Pennsylvania, 1972

Statues of the Four Unknown Bowlers, each on the verge of ecstatic release; a vast domed interior; a single towering entrance; a steep bank of steps serving to expose and separate out the weak and infirm: this citadel of pure athleticism is Speer at his most visionary—and least practical. "All's we wanted was a roofing job and a new sign," huffed vexed Bowl-O-Rama proprietor Mel, "and this nut in a trench coat comes up with a Taj Mahal!" Speer later tried selling the same plans—Unknown Bowlers converted to Unknown Carpet Layers—to the House of Shag down the way, but again without success.

GONE BUT NO

CANARD-ET-CHICANE BOMBER, DADAIST FREE SQUADRON, FRANCE

Not to be confused with the Artists & Models Escadrille, also born of patriotic desperation in the glorious hopelessness of May 1940. The Dadaist Free Squadron flew its own Canard-et-Chicane 607-B, bought from L'Armée de l'Air via a crooked cabinet minister for 100 francs. The all-volunteer Dadaists' "nonsense tactics" of bombing French troops, carrying no bombs, or simply staying parked on the tarmac for days befuddled Nazi attackers and French defenders alike. But the true confusion was on board. Indeed, it was on May 9th over Arras, when a splinter faction of Futurists joined with the Cubists and forced a vote on whether to keep flying or land, that the Free Squadron's valient career ended. The vote produced a deadlock, and after circling a landing field for hours, the Canard-et-Chicane ran out of fuel and crashed. It lives on today at a *frites* stand near a go-kart oval just outside Loos.

ORGOTTEN

AMALGAMATED B-888 "STRATOFLATTENER" BOMBER, UNITED STATES, 1953

Only one prototype of this 14-engine turboprop behemoth (note accompanying B-17, dwarfed by comparison) was ever built. The Stratoflattener superbomber never achieved its intended status; Senate hearings confirmed that the required crew contingent was too large to leave space for bombs and that training noise-deafened crew members to lip-read would drain the Air Force's budget. Mothballed in Arizona in 1954, the lone Stratoflattener gained a dubious new fame when it was started up at an Air Force Day celebration and triggered the Great Arizona Quake of 1959.

BODO + VULCH BV-901 NIGHT INTERCEPTOR, GERMANY, 1945

No substantiation exists for the legend that Adolf Hitler himself designed the BV-901, nicknamed Hummer (Lobster). "He wasn't that batty," debunks one ex-Luftwaffe officer. It was in fact designed by the freshman class at the Hermann Göring Trade School for Boys at Karlsruhe in the waning days of the war. Power came from seven different engines, on the theory that if even one or two broke down or exploded, enough thrust would be left to keep the Hummer aloft. Turning the school's bus, furnace, refrigerator, and emergency generator into engines of one ingenious type or another, the lads did their best, but the Hummer's trajectory was naturally straight down, so the Luftwaffe recommended using it as a bomb. The Frau Goebbels Girls' Home Economics School was racing to design a plane large enough to carry it when the Nazi air war ended.

HRABNY-CHUD "MUMMA" TRAINER, CZECHOSLOVAKIA, 1945

Secretly produced in a Prague tailoring plant during the Nazi occupation and powered by a single 56-cylinder engine made of 28 sewing machines, the Hrabny-Chud was slow and clumsy but *"nert hobny de zignat abagnad!"* (smooth as a sewing machine), according to those who flew her. Its unique modus operandi was: fly over retreating Nazi columns, stall, and make pancake landings on their hapless heads.

NAKA R-2 "MARYBETH" DIVE BOMBER, JAPAN, 1941

The carrier-based Marybeth was one of the most feared of the Imperial Navy's single-engine torpedo bombers—feared especially by its pilot. So nose-heavy that it automatically went into a vertical dive the instant it left the deck, the R-2 had to be carried aloft by a mother aircraft and jettisoned directly over the target. Alas, since the Marybeth was unable to pull out of the ensuing dive and plunged straight down into the sea, every attack became a kamikaze mission. The aircraft was withdrawn from active service in 1942. Marybeths spent the rest of the Pacific war on the home front and saw limited duty. There are still Japanese who remember pilotless Marybeths screaming earthward to crash deep into the ground, doing their part by excavating new building foundations.

PLOD 456 WHALE BOMBER, U.S.S.R., 1941

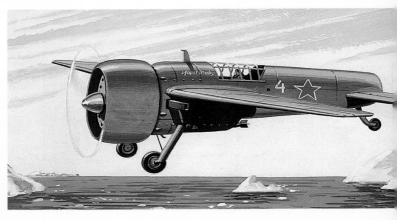

The besieged Soviet Union faced starvation in the dark days of late 1941; one desperate hope was whale meat. The Plod was designed and built in six weeks to spot and harpoon the great beasts, and for the next 18 months Plods plied the Black Sea in search of prey. Then— scandal. It was found that no whales had ever existed in the Black Sea. The Plod's designer vanished. Teaching of marine biology was forbidden. Whale exhibits were removed from museums, and it was not until 1972 that the Black Sea reappeared on maps of the Soviet Union. The whale is depicted as a mythical beast in Russian classrooms even today, and the Plod was so utterly erased from the annals of Soviet aviation that a longstanding suit before the World Court at The Hague by Jane's *All the World's Aircraft,* intended to force the files open, was recently abandoned.

SPIRIT OF KIM IL SUNG 2R7-6 PHOTO-RECONNAISSANCE AIRCRAFT, NORTH KOREA, 1968

The 2R7-6's absence of windows marked an extreme expression of the notorious North Korean fetish for secrecy. The aircraft was designed to overfly many vital South Korean sites classified as top secret, but pilots could not be trusted to see such areas themselves. Thus a blind-flying pilot was forced to snap pictures by hoisting a handheld camera up through an overhead hatch at the exact split-second he was ordered to do so by radio. Almost as bizarre as the 2R7-6's lack of fenestration was its "Sweet Breath of the Leader" steam-jet engine, which regularly iced over at high altitudes and sent the craft hurtling earthward. This explains references in North Korean propaganda organs to "Dear Kim Il Sung's 'Let a Thousand Icicles Fall' Miracle."

STOKELY & STARKLEY "UNICORN" FIGHTER, GREAT BRITAIN, 1939

Still noted for its role in the defense of Penzance—perhaps because Penzance never needed defending—the Unicorn was shifted in 1941 to the Middle East, where it was hoped that the unorthodox craft's frequent inexplicable prangs would distract Rommel's forces. The plan backfired after German propaganda boasted of all the ammo saved by not having to shoot down an aircraft entirely capable of destroying itself unaided. Splendid in intent and sincere in ambition, the Unicorn would play a vital role in the postwar world; the private papers of Lord Mountbatten reveal that it was Great Britain's gift to India of three squadrons of Stokely & Starkleys that clinched that nation's demand for independence.

BIXBY "MYSTERIOSO," UNITED STATES, 1940

This blurry snapshot is all that remains of the daring Bixby Mysterioso X-O prototype, still shrouded in rumor and controversy. The designer was Major Howdy Bixby, who continues to allege that his arrest as a Nazi saboteur shortly after this photo was taken reflected not fact but the American hysteria of the time. A special courtmartial hearing seemed to support the major, who was judged not clever enough to be a saboteur or an aircraft designer.

1. Third-class passenger Josephine Baker embarks for Cherbourg.

2. Demanding a larger stateroom, passenger Wallis Warfield embarks for Southampton.

3. Seven-year-old John F. Kennedy spies father, Joe Kennedy, smooching with Gloria Swanson.

4. Dutch Schultz threatens Legs Diamond in back room of Jimmy Walker's favorite speakeasy.

5. Sinclair Lewis punches out Theodore Dreiser in Edmund Wilson's living room.

6. James Thurber is asked to leave the Robert Benchleys' after drawing on the bathroom wall.

7. Edward Hopper hits on the subject of his next painting.

8. Georgia O'Keeffe two-times Alfred Stieglitz with Man Ray.

9. Lee De Forest sits in the living room watching Mrs. De Forest do the dishes in the kitchen in the first sound-on-film screening.

10. Filing his fiftieth Broadway gossip column, Walter Winchell blasts "high-hat British snobs like Duke Ellington."

11. Ernest Hemingway belts Zelda Fitzgerald after losing an arm-wrestling match with Jackie Coogan at Michael Arlen's.

12. John Barrymore takes a swing at brother Lionel as sister Ethel and the Lunts try to intervene.

13. Dorothy Parker freshens up her drink.

14. Theda Bara attends the world première of "The Gold Rush" and misses the Eleonora Duse memorial service.

15. George S. Kaufman meets Moss Hart when their taxis collide, injuring pedestrian Winston Churchill.

16. A correction in tomorrow's *Times* confirms that Sherwood and Maxwell Anderson are not brothers.

17. Commerce Secretary Herbert Hoover is heckled during his speech at the annual New York Stock Exchange dinner by a man identified as "F. D. Roosenfeld."

18. John O'Hara crumples up a letter from the *Smart Set* rejecting all sixteen short stories submitted.

19. Algonquin Round Table consigliere Alexander Woollcott blackballs the membership application of President Coolidge.

20. Houseguest Noël Coward suggests that Cole Porter change the title of his new song from "Rank and File" to "Night and Day."

21. Nine-year-old Orson Welles stars in his production of "The Tempest" in the family living room.

22. Jack Dempsey knocks out Tunney, Firpo, and Sharkey.

23. Queen Marie of Romania skips out on her hotel bill.

24. Fred and Adele Astaire celebrate their graduation from the New York Academy of Hoofing by dining with Jimmy Cagney.

25. George Gershwin ducks the opening performance of "Ziegfeld Follies" to rehearse "Rhapsody in Blue" for tomorrow night's Aeolian Hall concert.

26. Harold Ross puts the first issue of *The New Yorker* to bed.

OUR YELLOWSTONE VACATION

Bobby wanted to watch the *Diff'rent Strokes* rerun but Peggy had already seen it, so they switched to *Hollywood Squares,* but only for a few minutes because Ned made such a fuss about never getting to see the Rodeo Channel back home. The motel TV only had twelve channels—this was way out west in Yellowstone Park, after all—and after a couple of hours the one thing everybody agreed on was that that sucked. No MTV . . . no VH1, even.

Then the news came on, and there was only some religious show and a lame old movie western. Actually that was kind of cool. The western scenery in the background was awesome. And it had Indians and bears and a moose and close-ups of this huge bird, an eagle or maybe a condor, looking down on the cowboy camp from way, way up on a rock. Bobby said it was stuffed but Peggy said no, look at its eyes, they move,

it's real all right. I'd like to see one of those birds live. That would be the coolest thing. Then Ned said the news is over now, let's see what else is on, and they found this nature show all about caribou and their babies. Well, better than the phony-looking cartoon space battle and the infomercial about hair restorer that was the only other junk that was on. Peggy said let's go back to the western movie, I want to see that big bird some more. And close the curtains, Ned, the light's ruining the TV picture.

Pretty soon it was suppertime. They all ordered in burgers.

PART II

TRACING THE INFLUENCES

LUCKILY, INFLUENCES AND INFLUENZAS
ARE NOT THE SAME THING.

—ANONYMOUS

Cowboys, soldiers, lingerie ads—the artist traced compulsively as a boy, and this trick of copying while others were creating influenced his contemporaries and fellow students to give him a wide berth. Perhaps this explains his preference for art schooling by mail, where assignments could be worked on far from prying eyes. Thus he enrolled in the Famous Artists correspondence school in 1957, although dropping out before developing close relationships with Norman Rockwell, Albert Dorne, Stevan Dohanos, Al Parker, Austin Briggs, Peter Helck, or any of the other kindly big-name, big-money illustrators cooling their heels around the campus mailroom in Westport, Connecticut, waiting to pounce on the next postage-due portfolio of penciled girls in bras and girdles.

This may be as near as the artist ever came to a teacher, a mentor, an influence. (True, he and Jackson Pollock once shared a cab in New York City, but not with each other, and not at the same time.) Had there been a guiding inspiration at hand, it is doubtful that he would have felt the need to submit those scores of matchbook-cover "Draw Me" heads that constituted another art school's application form— or to bitterly hoard those scores of rejections.

Yet if so, what to make of the fact that among the effects recovered from the Paris attic where he spent the winter of '63–'64 (even though his lease covered an entire five-room flat) was a well-thumbed copy of *How to Draw French Animals the French Way*? Had he found a master worth emulating in the obscure person of a how-to-book teacher of barnyard anatomy? If so, it would appear to have been a testy relationship. Margin notes: "Camel not a French animal" . . . "Hogs don't have horns!" . . . "He can't draw the hind leg of a horse either!"

What is virtually certain is that De Kooning, Bacon, Braque, and Duchamp deny having ever known him or seen his work, despite all of them appearing on the back of the same American Express receipt from Tad's Steakhouse in New York City, charged to his account. Filling out fanciful guest lists for dinners he never hosted has long been a favorite pastime, as vouched for even by the Internal Revenue Service.

Nor from those acid-penned social critics Hogarth, Cruikshank, Daumier, and Nast did he appear to learn so much as a jot or a tittle. But then, how could he? Like so many other people, they are all dead.

MR. BUSH HAS A DREAM

Hello, this is your President talking.
Have I got an environmental plan for you!

My fellow Americans, as your President, my most trusted advisors tell me that real leadership begins by following their advice on what's good for America. I am happy to do so, because they also tell me that it's the best advice available. And frankly, that's good enough for me, which coming from me really means something, because I am, after all, the President.

The time for bipartisanship and civil debate is behind us. It's always easier to tear down than to build up, and that is why I'm tearing down as much as I can. Energy, conservation, preservation, the environment— let's do away with slogans and catchphrases and set national policy by *humbly listening* to the loudest voices.

These voices tell me that one of my dreams for America is to buy Oregon, rename it New California, and convert the "old" California into a maximum-security federal prison with a very tall fence around it. This will end the so-called California energy crisis, relieve our overcrowded jails, create thousands of jobs for screws and matrons and executioners, and save $383 trillion that will go toward a retroactive tax cut in the final weeks of my first term, allowing every American citizen to buy or lease the biggest SUV he or she can find—and incentivizing the oil industry to explore even in places where there is no oil!

It is also my dream—not the one featuring J. Lo, or the other one, where I win Poppy's respect by getting a C-plus average at Yale—to see new logging roads crisscrossing our national parks and nature preserves, maybe even your own backyard. Because wherever Big Lumber needs to go, *right now,* to turn those green forests into greenbacks for the political action committees that have brought our political system to the state it is in today, is as much a part of the American Way as wood. Or there would be no Popsicle sticks or baseball bats. In fact, even as I speak, surveyors from the Army Corps of Engineers are staking out the symbolic logging road to be hacked from one end to the other of New York's Central Park—too long a scandalously underutilized forestry resource.

And that's not all. We need to confront America's energy needs head-on with bold new initiatives, such as harnessing the nation's unemployed for human power to manually turn the wheels of the thousands of electric miniturbines and treadmill generators planned for installation in parks, picnic grounds, campsites, and other useless spaces nationwide, generating billions of kilowatts of free electrical energy to keep our video

Artist's rendering of the soon-to-be-completed logging road through
Central Park (with spires of Upper West Side looming in background).

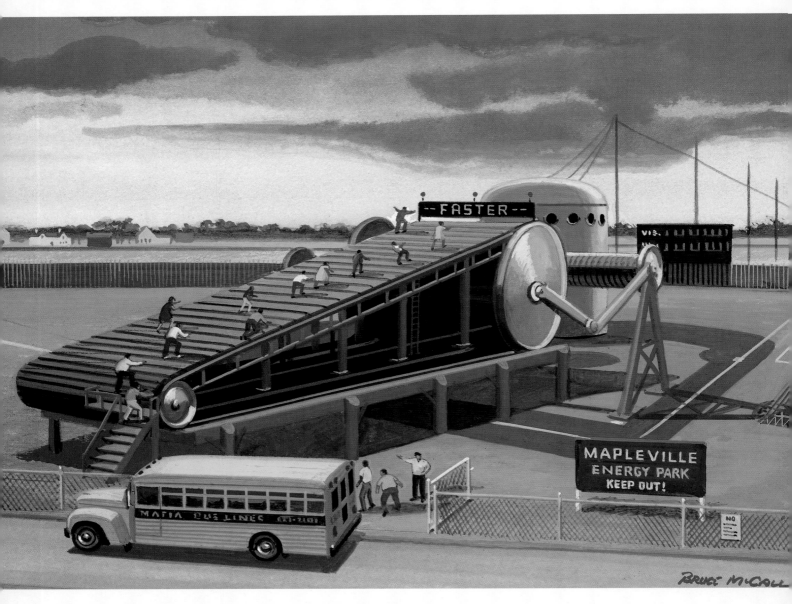

Say "No" to sloth! Say "Yes" to energy produced by the unemployed.

games, illuminated billboards, and shoe-buffing machines—our very lifeblood—humming. Think of it: The more homeless, unfortunate, and unemployed among us, the more free electrical power!

As your President, and, for that matter, mine too, I am told that I am dedicated to solving the problem of our increasingly endangered freshwater supply. Mere half-measures may suffice for civil rights and education, but not for this. *We must eliminate America's outdated fetish for fresh, clean water within our lifetime, if not sooner.* This would set industry free to turn every river and lake into the toxic brown sludge that says, loud and clear, "Costs way down, profits way up!" And it can be done, once our drinking and all water needs are met by the most plentiful and renewable water source on earth: tangy, sodium-, iodine-, and manganese-rich water from the sea. Try one sip: You'll want more, and more, and more.

And let's not ignore nuclear power. I think that's spelled "nucular," but statesmen can agree to disagree. The menace of a nuclear meltdown and runaway radiation, my fellow citizens, is exceeded only by the specter of giant utility companies being barred from using this cheap form of energy. That is why a national lottery should be conducted as the only fair way to assign the locations of all new nuclear power plants and waste storage facilities. My National Lottery Director, the former Secretary of State of Florida, reports that the results have come in even before the lottery has been held. Due to an amazing statistical quirk, she informs me that the states that voted Democratic in the last federal election will soon have a slew of nukes.

Finally, your President has our national wildlife refuges lined up in his sights. I intend to sign off as soon as I can find a pen on Operation PAVE (Protect America's Valuable Ecology), a program already mobilizing to cover millions of square miles of fragile tundra, grasslands, marshes, and other wildlife habitats with a protective six-inch coating of fireproof asphalt. The prevention of broken buffalo ankles, skinned moose knees, and cut grizzly bear paws through the elimination of all rocks, bumps, gopher holes, and other hazards of nature can only be imagined.

Gas pipelines, oil pipelines, water pipelines—I think of these as the varicose veins of the economy. And I am now set to augment them with a new *animal pipeline,* sealing our wild four-footed friends into an all-steel, 2,000-mile-long habitat to keep them snug and safe from the strip-mining, oil drilling, and deforestation that I plan to get going, toot sweet.

Now I am overdue for my nap. But I promise you, my fellow Americans, and all you foreigners out there who are not yet Americans: I will sleep better knowing that I have left it up to you to carry out my responsibilities. Good luck, and good night.

Inspirational conservation messages from our President, freshly chopped out of virgin
pine forests and visible from 20,000 feet.

Car Wash of the Gods, Hollywood, 1937

Champagne Lane was on Wilshire near La Cienega, and it was *the* Hollywood car wash. "The Car Wash of the Gods," they called it. They used champagne, that was the gimmick, and it was real champagne, though it was best not to snoop about vintages and such. Hitchcock told a haunting story about Champagne Lane. He was going through one day around 1946—toward the end, when just bums were working there—and this arm appeared wiping his windshield, then a head, and slowly, through the suds, Hitch saw who it was. It was D. W. Griffith. Brrrr.

Hollywood Memories

It was still a small town back then, like one of those medieval guild towns—Ghent, say, weaving celluloid tapestries in the sunshine. People felt good. The police took Wednesday afternoons off. The mayor of L.A. lined up with everybody else for a day's work as an extra at Habsburg-Vainglorious, way out on Melrose.

It was a deluxe life for picture people. Stars got passes that let them run red lights after midnight, for example. Red Vox, the cowboy icon, used to shoot out the chandeliers at that nightclub on Doheny with his big Colt .45. Not so much as a fine! People knew that picture folks had to blow off steam, because the pressure was unrelenting. Talk about "the show must go on." Get hold of a print of *Wings over Tomorrow* sometime. Chilling. Oh, they tried skirting around the fact that Vance Tremayne's left leg was broken, but watch his face in the dance scene, the grimaces. Haryce Le Trine did *The Singing Safecracker* with a fractured skull, which explains not only why she wore a nun's habit (in the role of a gangster's moll) but also why critics of the day railed so darn much against her.

But if it was a sweatshop life, it was a happy sweatshop, even for the much-maligned writers, who got famous, rich— and laid. You'd see a newly arrived writer, even a mole like Tommy Mann, wallflowering through parties—and suddenly the teeth would change, the tan would appear, along with the Sulka outfits. It was all "Please, call me Biff. Have you met Miss Musk?" The pictures brought out Dreiser's flair for screwball comedy, gave H. G. Wells a whole second career as a script doctor, won Bunny Wilson an Oscar for *Manhattan Hayride* in '36. So, please.

Dark side? Well, exploitation. Actresses who wouldn't take off all their clothes had no chance. Actors had to bring their own guns, horses, what-have-you. Rule Hudshaft, casting director at First-Zoetrope-Zang, made people do the hula or eat newspapers in auditions because he knew he could humiliate anybody in return for giving them work. Rule was scum. So was Zoltan Esterhazy, the director. The bastard actually hanged two extras in the lynching scene in *Bullets West*—then did a reshoot because "it didn't look realistic enough."

But these were the rare bad seeds in the Hollywood pod. It was a family. My God, even Ferma Dobray would put down her famous opium pipe promptly at five on Sunday to go to the even more famous strawberry social at the Schlucks'. Executives, actors, extras—everybody would race off at lunchtime to the Motomat, on Robertson. Two on a motorcycle racing around that little figure-eight course, the one on the back picking off bags full of hamburgers from the hands of cast-iron jockeys. Or trying to; the fun was in the near impossibility of it, you see.

Meyer M. Meyer, the head of Pictograph, never lunched at the Motomat. Pathologically cheap, he'd eat in the studio commissary kitchen. He was the originator of that famous phrase "Smokink costs me nuttink," from his trick of lighting up a rolled $500 bill and smoking it down to just this side of the halfway point, then sending a minion to the bank for a replacement. Hired women to watch him lick fur coats, something unresolved from the old Odessa days. A strange man, Mr. Meyer. "Vatch de popcorn," he'd say. He knew that if moviegoers ate a lot of popcorn it meant they were bored.

Idleness was feared more than Mr. Meyer. Neville Blackguard—wonderful character actor, unjustly forgotten—used his time between pictures to become a brain surgeon. Alas, the malpractice suits drove the poor man to drink, which of course only brought more malpractice suits. He ended up so broke that he knew he wouldn't be able to afford a decent funeral when his time came. One night he just said what the hell and sneaked into Forest Lawn, dug his own grave, and jumped in.

And who says the town had no heart? The Forest Lawn people let him stay where he lay. And, though admittedly it was from the prop department and the name and dates were off, dammit, his old studio did provide Neville Blackguard with a headstone. Gratis.

Buddy's Fly-Inn, 1934

Jimmy Doolittle would zoom in for supper straight from the Pomona air races in that nasty little Gee Bee thing, and he never throttled back until the ship had run right up to the very top, whereupon he'd cut the motor and roll to a stop as easy as if he were parking a Buick. Jimmy wouldn't go in with Buddy on making a national Fly-Inn chain, but, you know, it had nothing to do with zoning problems or financing. The fact is that Buddy's kitchen—well, everything had that benzine flavor to it, everything tasted kind of smoked in an unpleasant way. And Jimmy Doolittle, if you knew him, he was a fellow who liked his eats.

BRUCE McCALL

Club Magneto, 1939

You entered Club Magneto in first gear, to give you a boost up the stairway. Spencer Tracy kept blowing the clutch on his Auburn and sliding back down every time. But if you achieved the foyer, so to say, *carumba!* The path, or road, or route, to your table snaked around and through the whole vast dining room, past everybody. Hi, David O.! Hello, Louis B.! It was a style parade, maybe more of a gauntlet, because your car and your presentation were being judged, mercilessly, by a cruelly unforgiving clientele.

Yet the consensus was that Zanuck tried too hard. He'd arrive with a fleet of matching cream-colored Cords: the scout car, his car, his flunkies' car bringing up the rear. Lupe Velez would roll in and then sit in the car for half an hour, an hour, while the wait staff cooled its heels and the margaritas got warm, whereupon, naturally, Lupe would throw a hissy fit and vamoose. Club Magneto was such an in inn, for a while, that you put up with the gridlock (except if you were Errol Flynn, who punched out poor Claudette Colbert once when their bumpers got entangled), and the lack of valet parking, and cutups like Bogart, who did things like hotwire Harry Cohn's Packard and roar around the room. Then Club Magneto went the way of all fads.

Wings Over Brentwood

Aeroboy, they called it. Hot meals delivered pronto, by low-flying planes based in Burbank. Not pizza or such offal, either, but haute French. You kept the silk parachutes for tablecloths. Howard Hughes was behind it, and the man himself flew lots of meal runs; many will recall seeing him in his silver Northrop Omega corkscrewing through Coldwater Canyon in that pinky L.A. dusk, heading for mogul Meyer M. Meyer's place and a dinner drop.

Gorilla Croquet at Fair Sigh, 1938

"Fair Sigh" was the Hollywood mogul Meyer M. Meyer's lame wordplay on Versailles, whose blueprints he used to build it. Fair Sigh occupied a vast oceanside tract north of Malibu; the croquet layout on the Great Lawn shown here needed cars to drive the players from wicket to wicket, otherwise they'd all be still out there under the moon. Gorilla croquet came about because Meyer had got stuck with this pack of gorillas he'd bought for a sequel to *King Kong* that he was planning, until the original *King Kong* people's lawsuit killed it. Zoos and circuses offered peanuts for the animals, so he just kept them. Damned intelligent beasts, too. They beat Meyer at tennis, at golf, and always at croquet. He started inviting his friends over on Sunday afternoons to watch them play on their own, against each other; God, the betting money that changed hands. If only the gorillas had known how much their wins were worth!

Hydraulica, 1928

There was something about Sunday brunch way up in the air that elevated the human spirit. People couldn't table-hop, you see. Western Union messengers just had to chill till you came down. No telephones. Heaven! And, of course, sitting up there on its literal and metaphorical pedestal, your car was the star. Nobody just ate and ran at Hydraulica. You lingered. Dusk became magical as the shadows lengthened and the blue of the night met the gold of the day and the Japanese gardeners' glee clubs filed in and wandered about below, singing Hawaiian songs of farewell and strumming their plinky little ukuleles. Maybe you were half woozy with mimosas by then, drifty-minded, and maybe some unexpected party invitation, or the sense that a romance was about to bloom, had you feeling that flushed, validated, so very Hollywood feeling. Nobody ever wrote a poem about the magic of hydraulics. Maybe someday somebody will.

A Remoteness Apart

The most unjustly forgotten hero of the U.S. Civil War lived a life remote from life itself. He had no home, no family, no place in the world, no name except a soubriquet conferred by others: "The Bird Man of the Chickahootchie."

Little is known of his life outside his two years of service in the Union cause. Even less has survived to explain his unique biological-ornothological origins, for as captured in an 1863 Daguerrotype, his only surviving likeness, this singular figure was irrefutably half man, half bird. A Union Army veterinarian's examination was cursory: "A poor specimen of a Man and a worse example of a Bird." Perhaps the mad urgency of battle obviated deeper scientific study. Perhaps, being half bird, he instinctively fled close scrutiny by man the predator. Perhaps. But evidence is strong that the Bird Man of the Chickahootchie was ultimately cast into history's shadowy periphery by man's innate fear and loathing and demonization of The Other. In short, by bigotry.

"We ever shoo him away from the campfire," boasted a fellow soldier, revealingly, in an 1864 diary entry, "wonting [sic] no truck with no g— d– *Feather Boy*."

The sketchy historical record has the Birdman first fluttering into a Union camp on the banks of the Chickahootchie River in Tennessee in May, 1863, evidently drawn by the sight of hardtack crumbs scattered all about, and seized while flapping about inside a tent. He was made the regimental mascot and quickly learned, parrot-like, to speak a few simple phrases. His adaptability to human ways was close to phenomenal. "Picks a lively banjo tune with his strong claws," noted the regimental bandmaster.

But the so-called Bird Man's power of flight and acute vision soon destined him for larger undertakings: After two months he was commissioned a corporal and made an aerial observer. The promotion quickly paid off. It was the Bird Man, perched high in the pines overlooking Smickley's Farm, who first spotted Johnny Reb's advancing columns marching to turn the flank of the main Union force at Pentecostal Corner; the ensuing Battle of the Chickahootchie was credited with spiking Johnny Reb's whole Tennessee campaign.

The Bird Man's vital contribution never made it into dispatches. His meager reward was a handful of seeds tossed his way in the battle's jubilant aftermath. Indeed, far from being grateful, the military sneered. He lost most of his tail feathers to musket fire at Snidesburg, and in his most memorable act swooped into the Confederate camp at Cattle Crossing in September of 1864 and plucked the next day's order of battle clean out of General Gaylord's hands. Yet the next day, in a letter home, a sergeant huffed, "Its [sic] a d_____ shame that our great Army should so hang on the acts of a Bird Brain. The Boys would rather *cook* him than soldier with him!"

The faithful feathered friend continued to live in a tree come rain or shine, dodging the stones hurled by his tormentors, nibbling on his stingy daily half ration of half a biscuit, and served the Union as its eyes in the sky from Chickahootchie to Third Hogwallow and through to the end. No medals were ever forthcoming. After Appomatox the Bird Man was leg-banded and mustered out and flapped off into the forest gloom, never to be seen by human eyes again: a hero meanly discarded, a victim of man's cruelty to man, to birds, and particularly to half men, half birds.

EL RANCHO CORRECTO

Visit America's First 100 Percent Risk-Free Vacation Resort Experience

Safely situated atop a metropolitan office building so guests avoid any risk of an air, train, bus, or car crash while traveling to or from the usual remote resort location, El Rancho Correcto strives to make injury-, disease- and death-free vacationing a reality. Access is by rope ladder, to eliminate elevator mishaps. The compact half-acre of grounds is fully paved—no mosquitoes, no bug bites. Clockwise from the top left: The **MOUNT CORRECTO HIKING TRAIL** is permanently closed to prevent falls, tick bites, muscle strain, or predator attacks. The wild foliage at its summit— off-limits to guests— doubles as a mulch pile and is organically sprayed hourly. Visit **CLUB NO SMOKING** for a profanity-free evening of stand-up comedy and U.N. party jokes. Note that the **SAFETY SWIM POOL** features a lifeguard backing up the life-guard, a nonskid bottom, handrails, and an anti-drowning depth of just three feet. Maximum capacity: two people. The coin-operated, stationary, non-equine **HORSEBACK RIDING CENTER** eliminates the risk of falls, runaways, and horse-borne

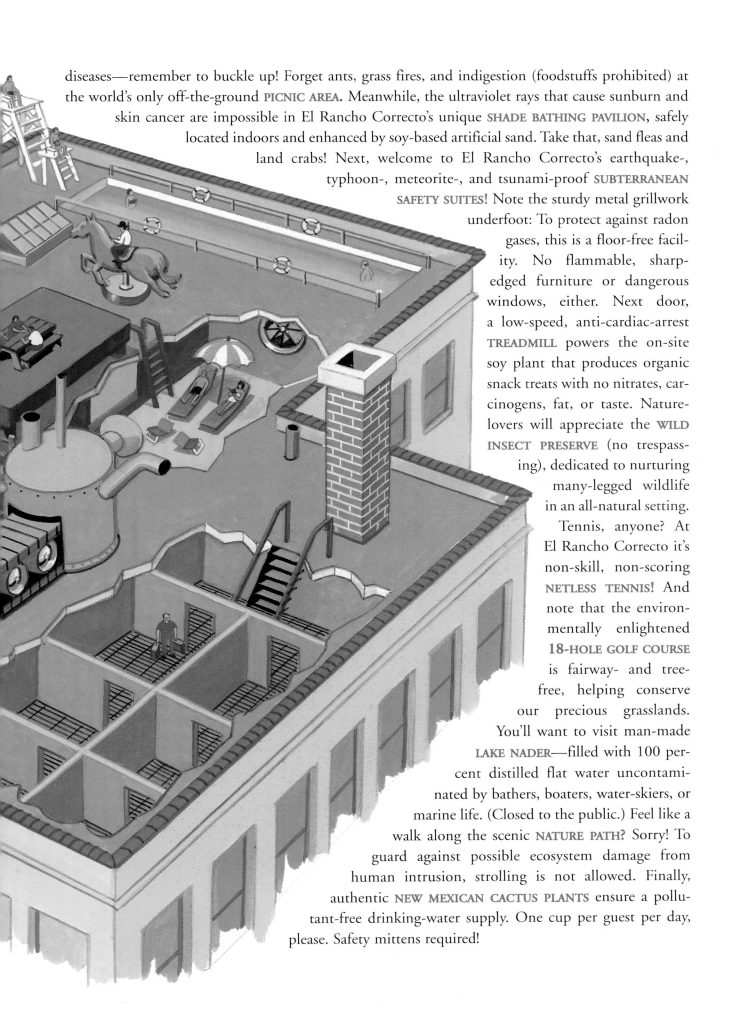

diseases—remember to buckle up! Forget ants, grass fires, and indigestion (foodstuffs prohibited) at the world's only off-the-ground PICNIC AREA. Meanwhile, the ultraviolet rays that cause sunburn and skin cancer are impossible in El Rancho Correcto's unique SHADE BATHING PAVILION, safely located indoors and enhanced by soy-based artificial sand. Take that, sand fleas and land crabs! Next, welcome to El Rancho Correcto's earthquake-, typhoon-, meteorite-, and tsunami-proof SUBTERRANEAN SAFETY SUITES! Note the sturdy metal grillwork underfoot: To protect against radon gases, this is a floor-free facility. No flammable, sharp-edged furniture or dangerous windows, either. Next door, a low-speed, anti-cardiac-arrest TREADMILL powers the on-site soy plant that produces organic snack treats with no nitrates, carcinogens, fat, or taste. Nature-lovers will appreciate the WILD INSECT PRESERVE (no trespassing), dedicated to nurturing many-legged wildlife in an all-natural setting. Tennis, anyone? At El Rancho Correcto it's non-skill, non-scoring NETLESS TENNIS! And note that the environmentally enlightened 18-HOLE GOLF COURSE is fairway- and tree-free, helping conserve our precious grasslands. You'll want to visit man-made LAKE NADER—filled with 100 percent distilled flat water uncontaminated by bathers, boaters, water-skiers, or marine life. (Closed to the public.) Feel like a walk along the scenic NATURE PATH? Sorry! To guard against possible ecosystem damage from human intrusion, strolling is not allowed. Finally, authentic NEW MEXICAN CACTUS PLANTS ensure a pollutant-free drinking-water supply. One cup per guest per day, please. Safety mittens required!

THE RISE AND FALL OF THE BUTTER TART

A brief but exhaustive history of Canada's premier patriotic pastry

1871: The Charlottetown Bake-Off is held four years after Confederation to establish an official Canadian pastry, thereby thwarting the dumping of cheap American mince pies. The judges, one from each province, initially pronounce a Manitoba-baked "liver loaf" the winner, only to have their decision vetoed by Prime Minister Sir John A. Macdonald, who rules that a liver loaf is not a pastry.

1873: The official-pastry issue is scheduled for debate in Parliament when a plate of small dessert delicacies, baked by the Prime Minister's cook/housekeeper, is gobbled up in seconds at the Members' luncheon immediately beforehand. Debate would be redundant; Canada has found its official pastry. All hail the butter tart.

1886: Bandits intercept a train hauling the first shipment of butter tarts to British Columbia from Ontario and destroy the entire 40,000-tart load. The Northwest Mounted Police quickly identify the bandits as mercenaries hired by the U.S. baking trust, triggering a Dominion-wide surge of patriotism that climaxes in Butter Tart Day, when every Canadian is expected to wolf down six of the goo-filled little treats.

1901: Her Majesty Queen Victoria is presented with a tray of butter tarts by the Canadian High Commissioner at a special Buckingham Palace audience. Shortly afterward, she requests the recipe and, never exactly sylphlike, swiftly balloons to more than 220 pounds. Within the year, she is dead.

1915: Canadian bakers co-operate to produce the world's largest butter tart, a doughy disc more than 30 meters in diameter, for display at the Panama-California International Exposition in San Diego. American customs officials turn it back at the border on the specious grounds that all imported foodstuffs must fit through the average kitchen door. Canada's official pastry is fated to remain Canada's secret.

1923: Butter Tart Mania sweeps the Dominion as a post-war sweet tooth spurs gluttonous consumption. Butter tart parties, butter tart clubs, poems and paintings featuring butter tarts proliferate. Kitchener, Ont., formerly Berlin, narrowly defeats a move to rename itself Buttertarttown. An American newspaper runs an article on Canadian butter tarts.

1940: Schoolchildren pushing wheelbarrows full of "inedible" Victory Butter Tarts march on Ottawa and force a return to home baking. Tonnes of uneaten government tarts will shortly be dropped over Nazi Germany in devastatingly effective pastry terror raids.

1969: Gourmand prime minister Pierre Elliott Trudeau spits out his butter tart at a state dinner for the Canadian international cribbage team. Butter tart consumption immediately takes a nose-dive.

1973: "Butter Tart Alley," that quaint, west-end Toronto street lined with butter tart emporia and butter tart-devouring throngs, is invaded by a doughnut shop of the fast-growing Tim Hortons chain. The industry newsletter, *Today's Canadian Butter Tart,* scoffs.

1979: There are now more Tim Hortons doughnut shops than there are butter tarts. The premier of Ontario, speaking at a dairyman's conference, decries the doughnut invasion that has wiped out 25 percent of all commercial butter tart bakeries in the past fifteen years. But his call for a mandatory "Not a Canadian Confection" tag on every doughnut goes nowhere.

1994: King Doughnut rules Canadian snack life as nine out of ten independent Canadian bakeries apply for coveted Tim Hortons franchises. At the annual Governor General's New Year's Levee, it is not butter tarts, but doughnuts, that are served.

2001: The first Canadian public-school history books in 128 years to omit all mention of the butter tart and its storied role in the nation's life are distributed to classrooms nationwide. No one complains.

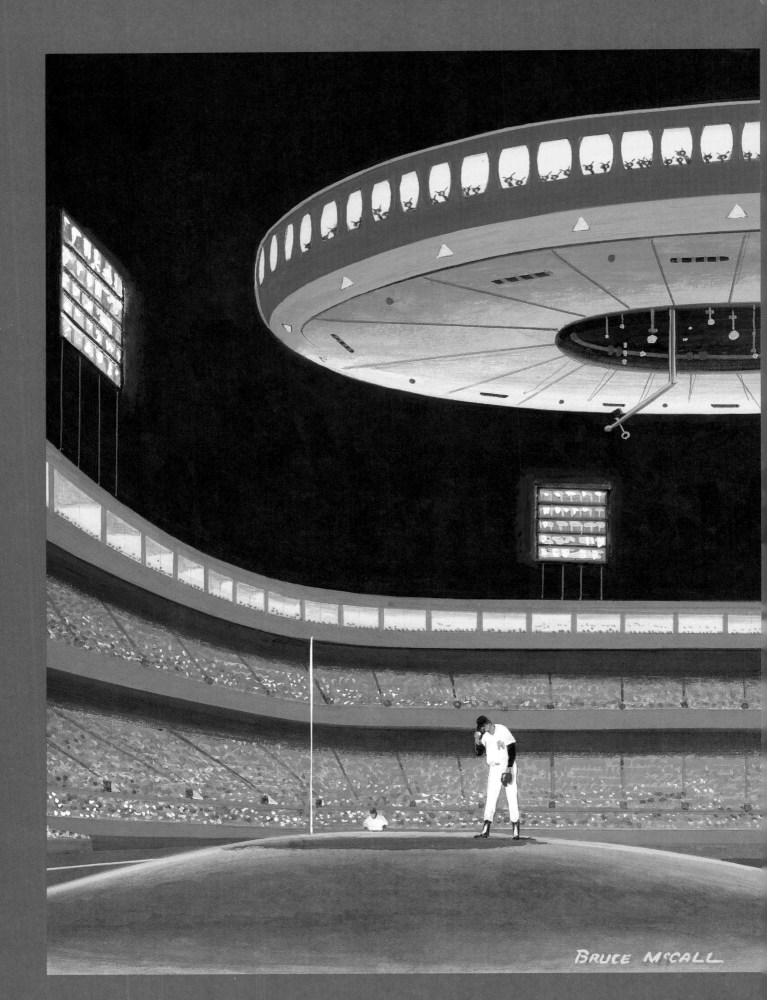

BRUCE McCALL

PART III

SECRETS OF THE TECHNIQUE

Versatility, the knack of doing several things well, is an essential part of every successful artist's oeuvre. This artist epitomizes that truth. For example, he draws with his right hand and throws with his left. He can hold a pair of scissors in his left hand and pare the nails on his right-hand fingers. He can eat peas with a fork or a knife. He openly laughs at those unable to rub their heads and pat their stomachs, or vice versa, at the same time.

The reader studying the images on the pages in this section will see only a series of pictures, giving scant if any thought to the aesthetic or manual dexterity, the legerdemain, in their creation. "It's all an illusion, you know," the artist twinkles. "Feel the page. Rub your fingertips around. See, that's not real sky, that isn't real pavement, those aren't real people. Everything you see in one of my pictures exists only as lines or smears on a totally flat surface. That's what made me realize those Flat Earth Society people are really on to something."

How does the artist achieve his miraculous effects of depth and movement and verisimilitude? Alas, that's a trade secret, insured by Lloyd's of London, but this much can be revealed: There are no hidden microphones, no mechanical table-jiggling devices, and no audience "plants." Those privileged to stop by his atelier have reported seeing no unfamiliar mounds of rare minerals, hearing no more than the usual everyday background din of hydraulic pumps, chain drives, and escaping steam, smelling no moldy earth smells. The artist seems to start with a blank surface and then steadily "fill it in," in technical argot. As a time-saving measure, almost every drawn line and brushful of paint ends up on the relatively tiny area of the picture itself—always on the front, never on the back. Call it superstition, but this artist never allows a picture to go out of his atelier until the paint is almost completely "dry," in the parlance. And just before it leaves, he signs it, often with his own name.

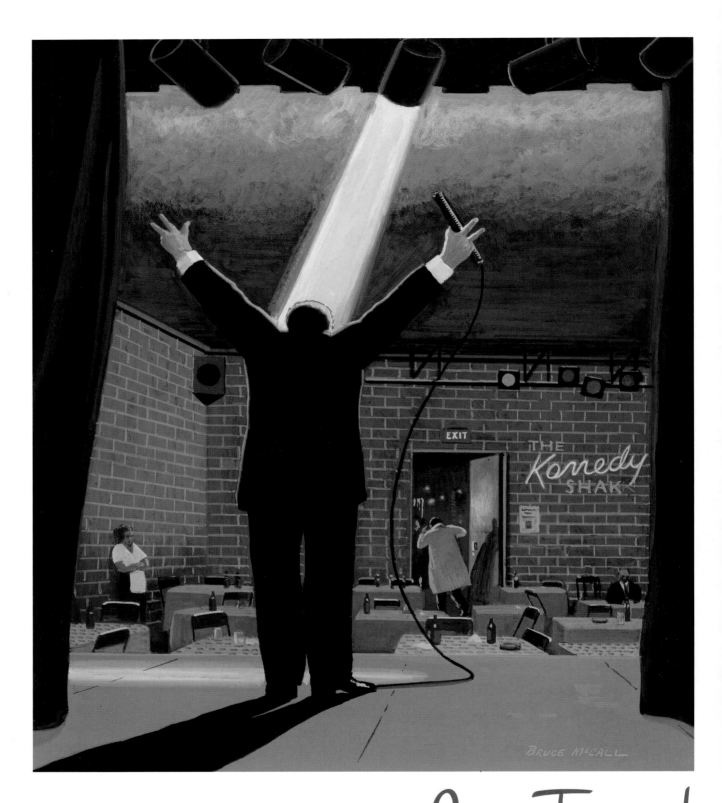

Richard Nixon: *Live Tonite!*

*Newly discovered tape reveals
former president's brief foray into comedy*

Now, I know you folks who come out to these comedy clubs are used to the high-paid type of funny fellow, the hotshots and headliners. Well, I'm not a headliner. Never played Las Vegas. That's for the good-time fellows, with the dirty patter kind of act. But that's all right. You don't get anywhere being bitter. You just work all the harder. Never afraid of hard work.

That reminds me, folks. I just flew in from Las Vegas, and, my fellow Americans, my arms are quite tired!

Okay. Of course if you think I'm not funny, that's your right. Constitutionally and so forth. I suppose some of you here tonight enjoy not laughing, because, you know—Nixon, kicking him when he's down, that's so popular. But let me say one thing, folks, and that's this: I'm not a quitter. Never quit. So those of you who didn't laugh, oh sure, Nixon's a stiff kind of comedian, not smooth like that Jack Benny fellow. Because, you know, I never had the big breaks. Couldn't afford the gag writers, never dated the showgirls. But I'm not ashamed of that. Never ashamed.

Now, this duck—I believe it was a duck—walks into a bar. And this very amusing duck, apocryphal duck of course, because ducks can't talk, this duck asks the barkeep for a drink of one kind or another. Let's say a martini. In any case, an alcoholic beverage.

You know, I've heard the boos before, the groans; in Venezuela in '58 they spit at my car. I'm used to insults. I've learned that if you stand for something—and I stand for something—you're going to get the insults, the disrespect. And you know, folks, boos don't bother me. They're your privilege as free citizens. But letting me continue, that's the American way, the democratic way.

So, this duck walks into a bar. A place of relaxation and I would say informality, very much like this comedy club here tonight.

And incidentally, you folks who supposedly came here for amusement, diversion—my mother would tell a joke of the week every Sunday. And when she told that joke of the week, you could hear a pin drop. Because of respect. Not some rich-boy joking-around thing. Respect was what I had beaten into me with a Holy Bible wrapped in a wet towel if I didn't laugh my lungs out at my mother's joke of the week.

But I'm not going to quit just because some of the people here tonight are part of the hate-Nixon crowd. I've been hated all my life—but you know, it's only made me stronger. And it makes me laugh at those folks who think it's funny, Nixon's funny-looking, Nixon isn't suave, not one of those slick fellows.

But what is it nowadays with these kids? Just the other day, a young person, long hair and no necktie, comes up to me on the street. Mr. Nixon, he says—[12-SECOND GAP IN TAPE].

I heard that. I don't miss much, you know. What do you call it, a raspberry? I've heard raspberries before. And I'd only say I feel sorry for the people who raspberry a dedicated American entertainer. Because they're the ones who are missing out. Now, some of you in the audience here, you're fine citizens. Fine Americans, who came here to hear me out and make up your own minds about is Nixon funny. But there will always be certain folks who say, oh, no. Got to shut him down. Prevent him from exercising his rights, because he's Nixon. You know, Nixon, the awkward one, the one who sweats all the time.

They say Nixon can't tell a joke. Well, I've got news for you. Nixon can tell a joke.

This rabbi, this priest, and this Polish fellow are on a desert island. Marooned there on a tiny, what do you call it, tiny atoll, in the Pacific. I know this, because I served in the Pacific in the war. Saw a lot of atolls. Probably more than any other supply officer in the Navy. They never mention that. Now as I remember it, the rabbi says to the priest—[38-SECOND GAP IN TAPE].

You know, you folks—yes, you there, I see you—you can walk out of here. That's your right. I won't beg and ask you to come back and sit down. Nixon doesn't beg. Never did, never will. Because if you beg, you're a weak individual that they'll walk all over. Ridicule you. But that's all right. If you can't take it, the ridicule will destroy you and they'll kick you around until—but that reminds me of the story about the traveling salesman and the farmer's daughter. A real hubba-hubba girl, as they say. Very shapely, you might say, well-developed for her age and so forth. Now this salesman fellow—[TAPE RUNS OUT].

Golf Carts of the Third Reich

Historians cite the 1938 Albert Speer Pro-Am Invitational as the moment when golf in the Third Reich began its long and eventful flirtation with mechanization, spearheaded by the rapid adoption and even swifter technological development of the self-propelled cart.

Played on Nuremberg's monster 270-hole Burning Foot course, with its vast concrete fairways and an average distance of 12.3 kilometers from pin to pin, the Speer Pro-Am venue gaudily expressed the Reich ideal of the iron-legged, long-ball-hitting German Super Golfer. But not for the first or last time, self-glorifying Party propaganda backfired. Imagine the Führer's rage when no one in his 26-man team could stagger through 21 days of rain and fog to make the final cut, forcing him to award Germany's most prestigious golfing trophy to an unknown Balt amateur. A quick response was expected from the Reichsgolfinstitut.

That response, of course, was the ZD-1, little more than a motorized collapsible bath chair, but the world's first mechanized golf cart, nonetheless.

The September 1939 outbreak of World War Two canceled that year's playing of the Speer Pro-Am. And by early 1940, Burning Foot had been converted into a tank-testing ground. But work on the ZD-1 and other cart types continued apace at the Reichsgolfinstitut's Augsburg "skunk works." It is also known that a slew of prototypes were demonstrated on May 9, 1941, to a wowed crowd that included Rudolf Hess. What made Hess, the next day, pack up one prototype and fly off to Scotland? To realize his dream of playing Troon? To peddle the golf cart concept to the British, as Goebbels' Propaganda Ministry alleged?

We will never know for certain. Beyond question is that the sudden vanishing of Hess and the prototype cart spurred a furious new burst of German golf cart technology—not only at the Reichsgolfinstitut but also in the military services, by personal order of the Führer. Now that the British had the secret, Germany must build an insuperable lead by working fast to outdistance them with new golf cart designs.

The rest is golf cart history, forged over the next few years in the larger story some call World War Two. The golf carts documented in this study are the heretofore unknown, unsung, unseen golf carts of the Third Reich, trundled out into the sunlight from half a century or more of hiding in the metaphoric musty shed behind Nazidom's shuttered pro shop.

Ladies and gentlemen, *meine Damen und Herren*—to the carts?

ZS-2 "SEA WEASEL" AMPHIBIAN, 1940

Operation Sea Lion, the Nazi master plan for invading England by way of a massive amphibian assault in the late summer of 1940, was a masterpiece of logistics and detail. Consider the diabolical mission of the Sea Weasel. History's first seagoing golf cart was meant to ferry a foursome of the crack Adolf Hitler Golf & Country Club Regiment across the Channel, drive onto land, speed directly to one or another exclusive English country club and there debauch its occupants, who would proceed to demoralize the island nation's golfing upper crust by their slow play, flagrant cheating (invoking the so-called Hitler Rules), and raucous behavior. Their beloved recreation ruined, the English pigs would quickly succumb. Rehearsals in the surf off the French coast, alas, revealed the Sea Weasel's fatal flaw: the four rear-mounted club-carrying canisters were exposed to saltwater. By the time the Sea Weasel had crossed the Channel, the woods would be soft and water-logged and the irons pitted with corrosion and flaked with rust. *Nein* to that, snapped the crack regiment's ace golfers. Operation Sea Lion—mercifully, for the sake of German golfing pride—was soon afterward scotched.

THE LIMOUSINE OF THE LINKS—
GÖRING'S PERSONAL GOLF CART, 1942

Fat Hermann had already cracked the chassis of the first four prototypes he sat in. Panicked that the Reich's number-one duffer was about to literally if inadvertently crush the golf cart program, Reichsgolfinstitut engineers decided that the best defense was a preemptive strike. They hurriedly fashioned this special cart around the Reichsmarschall's unique dimensions and presented it to him as a birthday gift, seven months early. Göring was delighted—and predictably enough, since *der grosse Luxuskart* radiated his baroque tastes and love of comfort in every detail. It was constructed on a sturdy railway handcar platform and fitted with dual rear wheels to support the combined heft of Göring and such on-board appurtenances as a hot-chocolate tank, a duck press, a boot-shining machine, and an inlaid mother-of-pearl tee caddy. Alas for Fat Hermann, the *Luxuskart*'s first and sole appearance was at his home course in the 1942 Carinhall Open. One glimpse and der Führer, tears welling, congratulated Göring for developing the one-man tank that Wehrmacht designers had failed to give him. He ordered it stripped of its luxuries and sent for testing to the Russian front. The fickle Reichsmarschall's sporting interests soon drifted to polo and the luge. Aside from an alleged sighting in Paraguay in 1948, later discounted, *der grosse Luxuskart* was never seen again.

BRUCE McCa

THE LANDCRAB—AFRIKA GOLFKORPS CART, 1942

Lightweight, agile, powered by a heat-proof, air-cooled engine, the affectionately nicknamed Landcrab was originally hailed as an ideal golf cart for the predominantly sandy courses of North Africa. Field experience reversed that positive initial response. Its designers were threatened with courtsmartial after the Landcrab's rackety engine noise was blamed for so abrading the nerves of Field Marshall Rommel during the prestigious El Alamein Open that he blew a gimme putt on the final hole of the tie-breaking round, allowing Italy's Marshal Badoglio to squeak through to a tournament win. Geared more for traction than for speed, the Landcrab was snail-slow: An estimated half of all units deployed were captured when golf-course traffic became so congested that there was no choice but to allow the advancing British to play through. Its lightness backfired in every sudden sandstorm; the other half of the Landcrabs lost in North Africa were classified as "Gone with the Wind." Within six months of its advent, the Landcrab was replaced in the *Afrika Golfkorps* by sturdily earthbound Bedouin caddies. All remaining units were returned to the fatherland and assigned to the Strength Through Joy movement to be used as motorized shopping carts.

THE GREENSKEEPER'S NIGHTMARE—
ZG-12, 1943

Legend has it that the gawky and cumbersome ZG-12 was developed by the Wehrmacht itself as a last resort after the Reichsgolfinstitut's design bureau had failed to produce a cart capable of carrying eight officers and their clubs over the notoriously steep and rocky courses of the Balkans. The truth is less savory—if more human. Enraged at being denied a Mulligan at every hole by his Reichsgolfinstitut partner during the 1942 Wolf's Lair Open, the Führer ordered the ZG-12 contract yanked from the Institute out of sheer choler. In any event, the Wehrmacht's novel wagon-and-trailer concept proved a bust from the moment it debuted in the Balkans in 1943. Partisans in the hedgerows were adept at chopping the chain that connected wagon to cart as the ZG-12 rattled past, leaving eight horrified golfers to watch helplessly as the trailer and their clubs rolled away. But the ZG-12 hardly needed partisans. It was its own worst enemy. Deployed on middle Europe's chronically soggy courses, the ungainly machine, with its giant tractor-type rear wheels, earned the lasting nickname of the Greenskeeper's Nightmare. "If the course is not muddy and ruined to begin with," wrote one embittered Undermower 2nd Class to his mother from Ruthenia in 1943, "it sure is after a ZG-12 or two has done eighteen holes." Scenes such as the one shown above—a ZG-12 abandoned by the road-side like an empty beer bottle—were all too common by 1944 as the retreating Nazis left scores of wagon-and-trailer units behind for the advancing Russians. Touchingly, in the only such gesture ever recorded in World War Two, the Russians gave them back.

ZENITH AND NADIR IN ONE—THE G-101 OZYMANDIAS, 1945

The tottering Reich was still capable of bold technological strokes in the spring of 1945, none more formidable than the Ozymandias—or, perhaps, more pathetic. The Führer, his head by now full of little more than an assortment of loose screws, was fixated on the fantasy of turning all of captive Holland into a golf course worthy of his gigantic ego, a course so vast that the distance between holes would measure in the hundreds of kilometers. To get in even nine holes in a day would require the speediest golf carts ever built. Thus the order to the Reichsgolfinstitut for a diesel-powered 145-mph "Mother Cart" with an 800-km range, carrying its own onboard clubhouse, pro shop, and 19th-hole bar. Capacity: 100 foursomes. Space was provided as well for a dozen smaller, pedal-powered satellite carts, to carry players from putt to putt on greens the size of San Marino. Only a single Ozymandias was built before the Allies retook Holland. Adolf only shrugged; his mind by then had become inflamed with plans for an amusement park with a mile-high, 300-mph roller coaster.

Z-262 ROCKET CART, 1945

When G.I.'s advancing across Germany in April 1945 overran the experimental golf works at Bad Schmell, Army corporal Bud Grogan of Ashtabula, Ohio, flung open the doors of a laboratory and there encountered a chilling Nazi revenge weapon, thankfully still only in prototype form. The Z-262 was a rocket-powered golf cart with one deadly purpose: to roar out of its hiding place in the rough at the posh Burning Foot course near Oberursel, captured by the invading Allies, and smash into the cart carrying supreme commander General Dwight D. Eisenhower as he pursued his favorite off-hours hobby. It would all happen so fast—3.2 seconds from takeoff to target, Nazi scientists estimated—that Ike's cordon of guards would have no time to react before their leader and his cart were blown to kingdom come. The sole Z-262 mysteriously disappeared amid the chaos of those final days of World War Two and was never recovered, though the baffling explosion of a golf cart at a public course in Ohio in 1949 has intrigued Army Intelligence ever since.

Pedalcabs, ornithopters, trolleys, and ferries in New York's immediate transportation future.

You've got to love New York City.

City Landmarks Commission calls emergency meeting.

Ice-level at the New York Supper Club Hockey League, 1938.

Crustacean bites man.

AIRPLANE STEEPLECHASE

Peapack, New Jersey, June 1934: Maj. Champ Starbuck in his U.S. Army Air Force Boeing P-10 leads Jimmy Doolittle's red-and-white GeeBee through the jumps in the challenging Piltdown Farms aerial steeplechase.

PART IV

THE CRITICAL CONSENSUS

NO CREDIT ON CREDIT CARDS

—STORE SIGN

The absurdist has never had an easy time of it at the hands of the critics. "It's absurd!"—like "It's a boy!" and "It's the Nazis!"—has a chilling effect on rational dialogue. Happily, this artist is not an absurdist in the classic sense of the term, nor, purely speaking, a surrealist, a Dadaist, or for that matter a seventh-day numismatist.

"Hack" would seem to arrow in on him and his oeuvre as do few other single words. Yet if by "hack" we mean someone of thin talent and flexible standards willing to do whatever is asked for the money, let us put up an asterisk after this artist's name, footnoting that in fact he has never critically savaged a children's dance recital for pay that did not, in the honest opinion of the payer, richly deserve it.

A hack, then. But not merely a hack, as these critical hosannas attest:

"... Adds a measure of crudity you don't expect, even from a hack."

"There are hacks, and then there are hacks, and then there's him."

"... The difference is, this guy actually enjoys being a hack."

But curiously, if not suspiciously, almost no critics have seized the opportunity to compare this artist's work with that of the Hudson River School, even though he has lived within four blocks of the Hudson for most of the past thirty years—much closer than many of the School's teacher's pets, mostly hicks from way upriver—and was the first nonstudent to dare ask if any Hudson River School alumni had ever gone on to postgraduate studies at the Amazon River School.

As, indeed, he was first to ask if brickbats are used in the game of brickball, since he has received so many and would be happy to donate them to a deserving brickbat team to make room for the stumbling blocks piling up in the hall closet.

BRUCE McCALL

The Hippest Cruise Ship on the Seven Seas

Got to love that black-on-black look! Can you make out the actual Amazon Rain Forest near the fantail? The Judy Garland Museum? The Zen retreat? The twenty-four-hour sushi restaurant? Meanwhile, D-Deck is entirely encircled by the Avenue of the Boutiques, with complimentary door-to-door limo service for Cocaine Class passengers. Speaking of which, you'll want to try crashing the world's only floating Eurotrash nightclub and disco, for all the good it will do! What you can't see in this view: The Rehab Therapy Clinic; the intimate twenty-two-person main dining salon, catered by Spago—sorry, invitation only; the 5,000-square-foot triplex Loft Suites with their own private screening rooms and, yes, veranda patios; and appearing tonite onstage, Mr. Bob Dylan! The hippest cruise ship on the seven seas: it's about time the ocean learned who really rules the waves!

OUR ENERGY-FREE
TRANSPORTATION FUTURE . . .

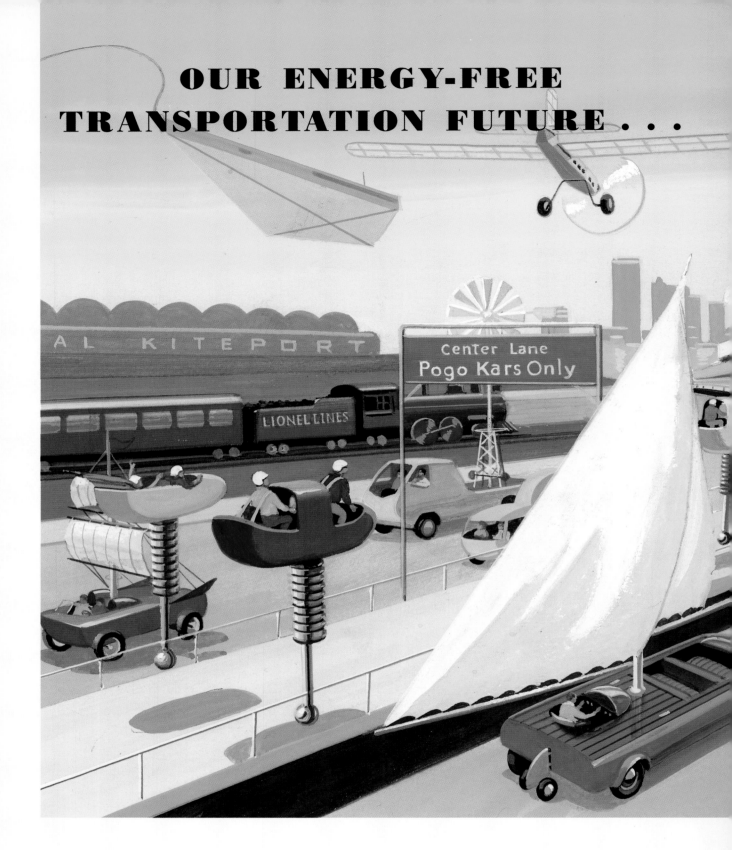

Here's a tantalizing glimpse of our post-Enron transportation future, heralding nothing less than a technological revolution in reverse! Good-bye fossil fuels, hello wind-, rubber-, and human-power! Out with dependence on foreign oil and greedy sheiks, in with total energy self-sufficiency!

Highways will come alive with the boing-boing-boing of sporty pogo kars and the steady brrrrrrrr of key-wound, clockwork-powered cars and trucks.

Spinnaker, an elegant custom-built sailcar, whooshes by, snapping and leaning into the wind, outpacing even the latest Windmiller JetStream Mark V.

BRUCE McCALL

There goes another Lionel Lines passenger locomotive spewing authentic-looking smoke. Overhead, a Trans-Breeze Airways kite plane wriggles upward, struggling for altitude. Hey, watch out for that super-jumbo Air Elastica Balsaliner coming in for a soft landing on gossamerlike paper-covered wings!

Sure, even with those towering wind-powered roadside fans helping to push us along, and countless Jiffy Twist rewinding stations to recharge wound-down springs along the way, we'll go a lot slower and get where we're going a lot later—but, hey, haven't we all been in too much of a rush anyway? And better yet, with each slowly passing mile, every American will be warmed by knowing that we're sticking it to OPEC—but good!

THE COMMERCIALIZATION OF SPACE

Some cornball sentimentalist decided that the U.S. and Russia should partner up in the first serious effort to turn a buck in outer space back in 2050 or so, since they were the two nations that had pioneered space exploration back in the twentieth century and all. So the two governments organized Space City, that tacky combination of a gambling casino and a football stadium. Of course the Russian Mafia took over the casino from the start, and the so-called NASA Bowl game, meant to be a kind of super-Superbowl, got all tied up in legal and broadcast hassles, and so the one NASA Bowl ever played ended up being

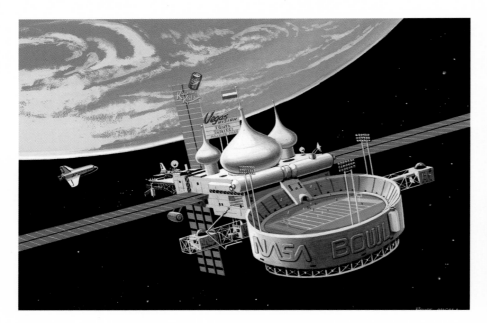

between two high-school teams from Texas. They had about 150 people in the stands, bouncing around in their space suits, tethered to the bleachers, and every time a kicker tried a field goal, there went the ball, over the Bowl and off toward the Crab Nebula. The hulk is still circling out there somewhere, empty and forgotten.

Whereas those poor bastards from the U.S. Department of Agriculture, marooned on the moon for their five-year stints sodding the place and trying to grow crops, were so bored that the sharpie who came up with Space Acres made a fortune overnight. It's always night in space so showings were 24-hours-a-day continuous, and being away from Earth for so long, the moon crowd was happy watching movies from years before. All new to them! Pretty soon the moon was surrounded by rocket-in outdoor movie theaters. Of course, like all fads this one faded after a few years, and once the first virtual brothel opened on the moon, the movie in lunar orbit as an entertainment form was dead.

THE WORLD'S SEVEN NEW TRAVEL WONDERS

Here they are, as chosen by the Official International Sightseeing Selection Committee, that anonymous, secretive, some say tyrannical but unquestionably all-powerful group of self-appointed Benelux-based bureaucrats, fresh from five cholesterol-packed years of globe-girdling junketeering and gift sorting—the Seven Wonders of the Travel World for the new millenium. Let's ignore the instant critical hailstorm, the ugly rumors, the travel industry's own lawsuit just filed with the World Court at The Hague, bandying buzzwords like "nutball," "idiotic" and "suicidal" in its attempt to overturn the committee's choices. The O.I.S.S.C. has rendered its verdict on the seven absolute must-see wonders of the travel world. So stop quibbling and start packing.

MUCHOPATIKA, LOST CLOUD CITY OF PERU

Fabled Muchopatika sits not only in but also actually on the heavy clouds swaddling the peaks and valleys of a remote section of the Andes. Scant wonder that this travel wonder—impossible to drive or hike to, so constantly windblown as to make frustrated cartographers weep, so "creepy," as even the ancient Incas put it—has long been wreathed in obscurity. Accordingly, little is known of everyday Muchopatika life, although a note in a bottle was found in 1948 announcing a complimentary welcoming cocktail and 25 percent off on all hotel bookings. Whether the offer still stands remains tantalizingly moot.

REVERSIBLE FALLS, SNAPDRAGON, WEST VIRGINIA

Awonder of hydraulics and water-flow management without equal in the known world, this 245-foot man-made waterfall can, with one brisk tug of a lever, reverse its flow and send thousands of tons of water cascading uphill. The falls was blasted from a mountainside in 1933 by the Army Corps of Engineers as the solution to a unique irrigation problem; precisely what the problem was has long since been totally forgotten, making Reversible Falls a double wonder.

THE VILLAGE THAT NEVER SLEEPS, FRANCE

Its haggard and snappish residents are the last persons to ask about the perpetual insomnia that makes life in tiny Trouf-sur-Ladoge, in southwestern France, a wonder of the world. Look instead to the railway suspension bridge vaulting overhead—the so-called Singing Bridge, built in 1987 and a wonder in itself. An ordinary bridge, as bridges go, but hear the wind whistling through its cables in an otherworldly and uncannily pitch-perfect rendition of the late chanteuse Edith Piaf's "Vie en Rose" day and night, night and day, year in, year out. Heard enough? Time to move on, and to roll up the car windows against the hollow-eyed Trouf-sur-Ladogians begging to come along.

NATURAL SINK, WESTERN AUSTRALIA

Prankish Mother Nature carved this freakishly convincing giant kitchen sink out of the local carbonated-hogstone scree more than 45 million years ago. Now, the Tourism Council in the outback settlement of Flat Baking Hell is pulling out all the stops to make the Natural Sink the Antipodes' new sightseeing mecca. For example, the first visitor to climb down and roll the natural sink strainer back into the natural drain hole wins $100 cash (Australian)!

THE INN OF THE FOOTSORE SAMURAI, JAPAN

Its breathtaking scenic majesty, its Zen calm and its exquisite raw chipmunk soup are legendary. But what most sticks in the minds of guests at the Inn of the Footsore Samurai is the memory of trudging up that steep muddy trail in their waterlogged shoes in the misty rain and the rainy mists, seemingly up to the heavens themselves, and of dragging heavy bags behind them every stumbling, lung-bursting step of the way. No breach of gracious Japanese hospitality, this; rather, it is ancient tradition that forbids the Inn from employing porters or bellboys, and has since the day in 1303 when its baggage carriers committed ritual seppuku en masse rather than surrender to an attacking samurai lord. Reservations always available!

OLD OPERA HOUSE, POINT AGONY, ANTARCTICA

Every schoolboy knows the saga of the 1910 Finnish South Pole expedition that lost its way, became marooned, went mad and decided to build an opera house. Few schoolboys—or even their teachers—realize that the opera house still stands, a glittering neo-Gothic edifice that took 14 years and 62 million hand-rolled snowballs to rise above the windswept nothingness, just a thousand-mile stroll across ice pack, crevasses, and mountain ranges from the nearest fjord. The next all-inclusive package-tour-cum-repair-party leaves in January. Bring mittens!

WORLD'S DEEPEST SWIMMING POOL,
AFRIKAAN SANDS HOTEL, SOUTH AFRICA

Here's one for the guidebooks: an inland resort hotel where the amenities are posh—and where heart-stopping excitement can strike at any moment! Carefree bathers plunging into the oversize, hundred-foot-deep pool for a refreshing dip will find the water clear and the shadowy shapes gliding in the depths far below pulse quickening. But the most carefree bathers by far are those who religiously refrain from splashing, thrashing or carrying meat.

BRUCE McCALL

WHAT'S WRONG WITH THIS PICTURE?

BRYCE McCOLL

Score 100 if you found the following mistakes:

1. The large building is not zoned for a drawbridge.

2. The autogiro lacks a registration number.

3. The boat has no oars.

4. The abandoned blue Citroen 2CV is illegally parked on private property.

5. There are no giraffes in this part of France.

6. This is not France.

World's Shortest-Lived Comic Strips

Renovation of Daimler Chrysler Building Almost Complete

Addresses of the Gods

000 FIFTH AVENUE

It says oodles about this co-op board's civic clout that Big Zero is actually situated on Park, and that it remains the only Manhattan apartment building whose basement has been featured in *Architectural Digest*. But disregard those "reign of terror" stories you may have heard—the board does reserve the right to rename dogs, but whether or not to divorce your spouse is almost always largely, if not entirely, your call. Outstanding feature: lobby mug shots of tenants with overdue maintenance checks.

THE CUSTER

lack of eastward-facing fenestration attests to the nasty prestige war Fifth Avenue that was under way when this Central Park West high-opened, back in '29. Still a quirky building: The 11 P.M. curfew and the cy dictating that guests must use the tradesmen's entrance irk just about rybody. But walk-through fireplaces and your own belfry somewhat pensate. Outstanding feature: General H. Norman Schwarzkopf (Ret.), t doorman.

700 ½ PARK

ltors angling to one day hook this listing 't come out and say so, but nobody has bid successfully for space in this nine-y alabaster fancy, the only known collab-tion between Stanford White and the ry chef at Delmonico's. Pass on 700 ½ if don't have a big family—these nine sto-form one apartment. What would you be ng to pay for great N., W., S., E. views, chmg rms, 24 fplcs, 148-car gar, etc., etc., ? It's not enough. It's not nearly enough.

COASTAL HOUSE

Stuffy plus—even mail from Madonna and her ilk is rejected from this property. Still the sole New York apartment building to charge for elevator rides and the only one whose super sits on the board of six Fortune 500 companies. New money is more welcome than old (viz., Page Six's sob-story item when Steve Jobs's new billiards room put the Dowager Empress of Romania out into the snow). Outstanding feature: the blood oath required at closing.

A TRENDSETTING FOLLOWER

IT'S A SIN TO SPEAK ILL OF OTHERS, BUT IT'S SELDOM A MISTAKE.

—OSCAR WILDE

It has long been this artist's contention, borne out by his career, that following trends is far harder than setting them. Happy the trendsetter, free to roam unencumbered on the wings of inspiration through virgin imaginative forest where no fad has gone before, knowing nobody is ahead of him. Pity the follower, blindly tracing a preblazed path and never daring to deviate from it in a humiliating game of monkey-see, monkey-do.

All enough to crush the most vibrant creative spirit. Providential it is, then, that this artist's creative spirit arrived already preflattened, extruded, and disassembled, and that freed from the outset of accusations of innovativeness, leadership, and vision, he so quickly found his natural groove, or rut, far from the glaring heat of attention and admiration that trendsetting can generate, making it so hard to see the drawing board.

To name a trend is to vouchsafe that this artist has followed it, or will as soon as news of it trickles down to his level. The topless bathing suit, pet rocks, Vietnamese cuisine, mutual funds, homeboy clothes—if these strike the art connoisseur as odd trends for a painter to follow, this painter could not more vehemently agree. Yet withal, preferable to trends in the art world. "They're exactly what you're expected to follow," snaps the artist, whose career has been about—if it has been about anything, the jury has requested a clarification of "about"—defying, nay, disappointing the expectations of others: his family's expectation of three squares a day; the car wash's expectation that he will keep hands off the "For a Rainy Day" can; the stop sign's expectation that he will obey its order, as unambiguous as the artist himself.

Or is he? Opinions differ. It is no simple matter of black and white. Arguments can be made on the one hand and then again on the other. What is important, in the end, is to consider both sides of the question, and only then decide. But as the artist always says to creditors, no rush!

THE RISE OF THE SKY

The quest for a loftier view has moved not only wealthy American sports fans in our time but the rich and the powerful from time immemorial. The so-called "skybox," i.e., a structure affording a privileged overview of an event or simply a vista, usually accompanied by lavish hospitality, probably first appeared as long ago as 3000 B.C. in ancient Babylon, or Babylonia (but never Babylononia). Archaeologists have recently excavated the ruins of a towering column of painstakingly stacked flat stones in the bleak Valley of the Bumps, estimated to have once stood 200 feet high. Shards, trinkets and an intact beer mug found at the site confirm that the tower was built to afford Babylonia's royal fans a king's-eye view of the quasi-religious vase races frequently staged in the semi-sacred Valley. The kingdom's strongest if not always brainiest menfolk would roll giant vases, jugs and other vessels from one end of the Valley to the other, over a rough-and-tumble obstacle course of rocks and gulleys and agonizingly steep grades. A shattered vase meant one limb boiled in oil, a lost race, a swift exile—but to the victor went The King's Sandwich, forerunner of that delicacy known today as the Dagwood. The world's first skybox, according to contemporary texts, fell or was pushed down by disgruntled vase racers around 2780 B.C. and was never rebuilt. Other texts suggest that vase racing had by then died out as a popular sport, eclipsed by the pastime known as war.

BOX

THE SKYBOX AS FREEDOM FIGHTER

C.I.A.-erected somewhere in the Florida Everglades in 1961 under the cover designation of a weather station and stuffed with every known electronic monitoring device, this round-the-clock eye and ear on Castro's Cuba is the world's highest (35,000 feet) skybox and thus (note icicles!) the coldest. It is unquestionably one of the most audacious feats of structural engineering ever undertaken, but is reportedly much dreaded by the crews who must endure a five-hour elevator ride up to the cramped little aerie swaying sickeningly in the jet stream, warmed only by a tiny space heater and conducive to serious attacks of cabin fever. The exact nature of the surveillance activities conducted from the skybox-cum-spybox is, of course, classified, but it's a no-brainer to conclude that one such is monitoring Cuban cigar output by measuring the smoke density over the island, especially after formal dinners, banquets, weddings and births. Scuttlebutt has it that the C.I.A. augments its budget by selling CDs of Buena Vista Social Club performances recorded via high-powered microphones.

THE NAUGHTIEST SKYBOX

Roly-poly North Korean Dear Leader Kim Jong II's hobbies are officially listed as model railroading, philately, and cribbage. The Great Architect of the Galosh Miracle's fascination with babe-watching goes mysteriously unmentioned. Yet why would the Steadfast Helmsman of the Anti-Fascist Swine Flotilla order a platform built atop his Pyongyang palace, have it directly facing the North Korean Young Women's Athletic Dormitory and hand out promotions and medals to the army officers bringing him high-powered binoculars with infrared lenses? What else could it be but yet another slander by the Capitalist Running-Dog Lackey Stooges?

THE MODERN SKYBOX
ERA BEGINS

A tiny maintenance corridor in an upper section of Philadelphia's Shibe Park was converted in 1938 by the advertising mogul and Athletics super-booster Clyde Lardbody into the first known stadium skybox. Lardbody enjoyed a sweeping view from his private vantage point, but the combination of his 300-pound bulk and the narrowness of the space meant that nobody else did. Invited (read "ordered") out to the ballpark by their boss, his top executives were left to spend the long afternoons sweltering and sulking in the claustrophobic gloom of the passageway behind him. The corridor-cum-skybox was abandoned on Lardbody's death in 1954 and eventually sealed off; from then until Shibe Park was demolished in the '70s, legend had it that half a dozen advertising executives were still sealed inside but too enervated to cry out for rescue.

THE SKYBOX IDEAL PERVERTED

As was all too graphically demonstrated by the late Royal Himself-for-Eternity General Admiral Ozo of the tiny, mud-rich African nation of Ozo-Ozo, the commanding view and personal privacy of the skybox can be bent to evil purposes. The self-declared National Savior Deluxe ordered the tallest freestanding structure in west-central Africa erected to overlook the vast and verdant grasslands near the capital city of Ozopolis in 1979. Picking and choosing from his personal arsenal of Soviet-supplied military weapons, General Admiral Ozo daily blasted away with automatic rifle, machine gun, mortar and rocket-launcher at every living animal in view as aids kept count; indeed, so consumed did he become with decimating the indigenous gazelle, giraffe, springbok and zebra populations that all governement activity virtually ceased, Ozo-Ozo's fragile economy stagnated and the Air Force, unpaid for months, mutinied. Ironically, it was the Air Force's Soviet-built tank—aircraft being redundant in a nation without an airport—that attacked and toppled history's most lethal skybox one morning in 1982, with the Royal Himself and his retinue in it. Ozo-Ozo is now known as Airforcia.

THE SKYBOX AT ITS SOCIALLY USEFUL PEAK

Students, graduates and Old Boys from England's best public schools built and furnished countless private skyboxes along the white cliffs of Dover in late summer of 1940—not merely to spectate at the Battle of Britain raging overhead, but to lend school chums and classmates now piloting Spitfires and Hurricanes against the Hun their fervent emotional and moral support. "It kept one muddling onward," recalled one Etonian RAF ace, "to see one's school colors and all the chaps and laddies from one's Form cheering and waving. And I say, how very offputting for old Fritzie!" Pictured here is the Spitfire of Flight Lieutenant Taffy ("Toffee") Fotheringham, Harrow Class of '43, of Winchester, Rugby and other schools.

MUSSOLINI'S SKYBOX

The Italian Duce Benito Mussolini, figuratively riding high as dictator of Italy in the late 1930's, literally rode high in public as seldom as possible. Heights reduced the blustering superman to a dizzy, rubber-kneed blubberer. Small wonder he preferred the solidity and safety of a balcony when addressing the adoring throngs. But when young admirers at Rome's Fascist Technological School built a telescoping one-man skybox rising at full extension to 100 feet above the ground, Il Duce was trapped: reject it and reap scorn; accept it and risk a grisly spectacle in full view of the assembled multitudes. Mussolini swallowed his fears for the sake of his image, and on All Fascists' Day in June 1938, gripped the railing tightly as the rig lofted him up and up above the Plaza of the Blackshirts. It wasn't the vintage Mussolini up there preening and pouting. He spoke in a low mumble, with frequent long pauses. Onlookers remember him often sagging and sinking to his knees. And then the inevitable happened. The official press statement spoke only of Il Duce "showering the People with the gift of everything in him." Mere hyperbole, some shrugged. But those caught standing immediately below knew exactly what it meant.

MEDICAL MIRACLE

The Doctor's Waiting Room of Tomorrow!

No more stares from that certified zombie two feet away. The end of the "Incredible Vanishing Receptionist." Of pleading for a cup of water. Of time standing still while you sit feeling as forgotten as *The Man in the Iron Mask.* Here's an exclusive look at the revolutionized doctor's waiting room that is every patient's dream.

BEFORE

KEY FEATURES

1 Sunken Receptionist Isolation Station in center of room. She can't sneak away!

2 Individual Patient Privacy Nooks with built-in television and cell phone.

3 Hand-held zapper gives doctor **4** a mild electric shock to the pants if your wait exceeds time posted on **5** electronic wall banner.

6 Seven-hole putting green.

7 Doc's Bar lets patients wet whistles—all paid for by Medi-Nip!

8 Free loan of best-selling books.

9 ATM machine.

10 Timer device frees up bathroom by automatically ejecting occupant after five minutes.

11 Comment board: rate the sawbones!

12 Strolling violinist replaces office Muzak.

13 On-site pharmacy/video store/newsstand/Lotto kiosk.

14 Running up-to-the-minute stock-market ticker.

REALITY CHECK

If it all sounds as if you've been dreaming—you have. Have a seat over there . . . the doctor will be with you in just a minute!

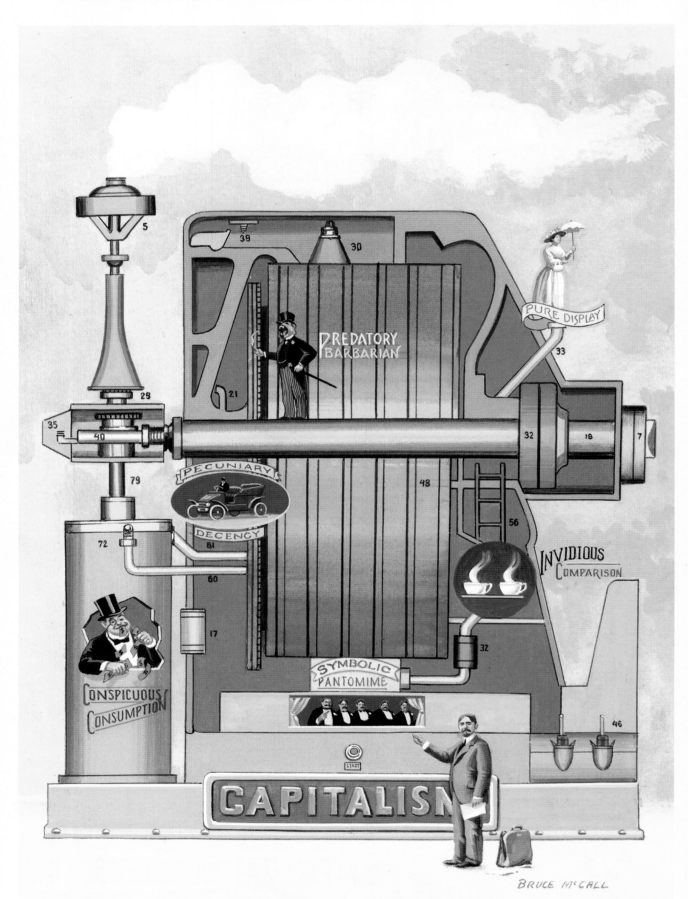

William H. Gates III initiates his custom of handing out a silicon chip to every deserving urchin he meets.

WORLD'S WORST GOLF COURSE

Giulianiland

Trumpland

PART VI

THE FUTURE OF THE INTERNET

IF THE ENDS DON'T JUSTIFY THE MEANS, WHAT THE HELL DOES?

—ROBERT MOSES

There comes a time, and it might very well be now, when analysis has served its purpose, when all the nuanced intellectual discussion of "the artist" and "the meaning of art" and other such top-lofty matters begin to grate and the mind's needle nudges toward Empty. If there was tantalizingly little to say about this specific artist and his work at the outset of this inquiry, that fact is now worn to a threadbare nub as these pages drag toward their—so mercifully close to the beginning in a book of this price—end.

So, how about those Yankees? Who has read the minutes of the latest Conference on the Laws of the Sea? Will New Zealand mutton discs ever catch on at McDonald's? More to the point—for the laws of perspective teach us that everything ends in a point—what of cyberspace and its effects on the way we communicate, relate, buy and sell our antique collectible galosh buckles? One world-renowned expert in the field has written what is perhaps the wisest commentary yet on the interface between man and the computer, too familiar to bear repeating here. Another, taking a passionately opposite stance, has yet to write it all down. But the changes being wrought by the Internet on you and me and Joe Lunchbucket cannot be ignored. Well, they can, but consider what you miss thereby:

An overloaded Pakistani computer crashes, killing 478.

A woman in Ohio named Dot Com slaps a $500 million mental-suffering suit on Silicon Valley—and wins.

The author of *Computers for Dummies* is revealed to have an I.Q. of 139; book sales plummet.

That man who barks "You've got mail!" from your e-mail message center is discovered not to be inside your computer at all and is not only miles away but isn't halfway small enough to get into your computer in the first place.

In short, there is plentiful room for disillusionment in this so-called modern-day panacea, not to mention an extra pair of hiking boots and a few Snickers bars. But it will be for the following generation to make corrections in time to divert the planet from hurtling on its certain course toward disaster. The spoiled little bastards have had a free ride long enough.

New York's Transportation Future Is Coming Tomorrow

THE SUBWAY OF THE AIR

Strung together like so many all-metal airborne sausages, "Zepp-Liners" such as these will by 1950 have succeeded subway cars, their Stygian tunnels long since flooded for fish farming. See the elevated platform towers standing so very high. Zepp-Liner punctuality and reliability will add billions to the City's economy by abolishing lateness and lost labor. It is meanwhile predicted that escaping the disease-ridden subways to breathe fresh air far above the treetops will extend the average rider's chest measurement by five inches and his lifespan by forty years. A passage from Staten Island to Poughkeepsie shall cost one mill in 1950 money, equivalent to a quarter-penny today. This reflects the happy fact that a provision in the Versailles Treaty obliges Germany to build four hundred Zepp-Liners by 1940, at a nominal price of no more than one cent each, and to maintain the fleet into perpetuity, gratis. So does the late Great War's glory reach forward into the future.

"Farewell, Father!" A subterranean pneumatic tube will shoot the commuter of 1950 from Nyack to New York City in seconds. Can you recognize the tube station pictured? Yes, it is a former manhole.

DINNER SERVED WITH A WHOOSH

Pneumatics will define smart dining in the New York of 1950. Orders will be placed by microphone and meals prepared in a vast central underground kitchen, then rushed piping hot to waiting restaurant patrons in seconds through a spiderweb grid of pneumatic tubes hygienically swabbed hourly. Pity not the waiters thus thrown out of work. Most were foreigners and, as such, carriers of malign Mediterranean disease.

THE RAIN CHECK MADE OBSOLETE

The New Polo Grounds atop Grand Central Station will hold more fans than all the other baseball stadia combined, though not at one time. And in event of rain, a giant umbrella standing in short center field will hydraulically unfurl in under two hours. Furled, the bulky obstacle directly in their path will challenge outfielders' ingenuity. Knowing best how lazy are baseball players, and stupid, the Club's owners may be forced to cut pay as motivation incentive!

1925 TO 1950: MASS LUNACY WILL BE TRIGGERED BY THE SUDDEN SHOCK OF CHANGE

But foremost phreno-futurists think that ice-baths can prevent the stress-induced explosion of vital nerve cells, if begun now. Those New Yorkers who remain sane shall dwell in a transportation Paradise of hydraulics, pneumatics, magnetics, and radio-naphtha waves, while eating in their sleep to save time. Ponder, too, the one-month pregnancy. And should muscles grow weak from lack of physical exertion, there will be a lozenge.

SOME LOOKS OF 1950

This ballplayer has X-ray goggles. Note bare feet.

Train conductor wears a powerful radio receiver.

Aviatrix costume will have a fur torso wrap.

A MAN-MADE ALPINE MIRACLE RISES IN CENTRAL PARK

A volume of earth equivalent to six Paraguays, excavated in the construction of the Manhattan-Montauk Tunnel, will by the year 1950 have been molded by more prisoners than there were slaves at the Pyramids into an artificial mountain in Central Park honoring our late President. All crags and promontories, home to the only grizzly bears east of the Mississippi and attracting mountaineers from as far away as Albany, the mighty cone called Mount Harding will rise so high that children standing at its peak will cry and gasp in the cold, thin air.

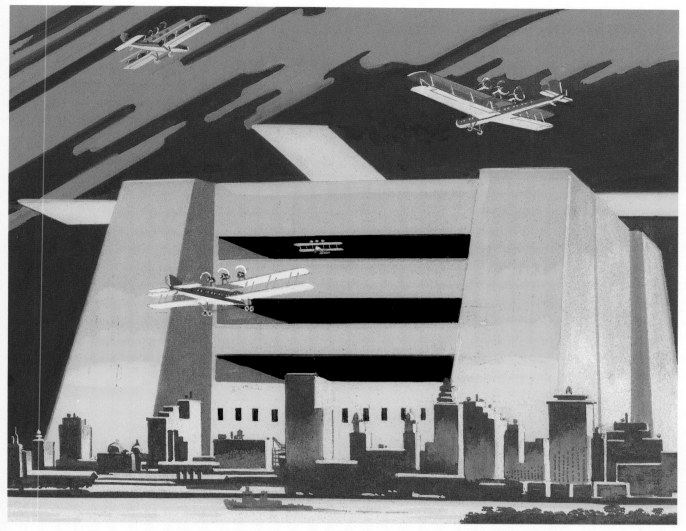

METROPOLITAN AIR DOCK: 12TH WONDER OF THE WORLD

The pressure of flight speeds above 160 mph would squeeze all blood from the brain and cause the memory loss called "Airnesia"; but the air wayfarer of 1950 will hang upside-down, bat-style, in special webbing, care-free. The twelve-motor steamship of the sky in which he hangs will have a veranda and a tuck shop. At New York City's Brobdingnagian ziggurat of Empyrian commerce, the Metropolitan Air Dock, aeroplanes shall land indoors, safe from chance collisions with farm animals, hayrick, and the like. The Air Dock's vast interior will house an aeroplane factory, Embassies of many nations, and, in its subterranean labyrinth, all Spanish tile and crepuscular light, a holding pen with capacity for two thousand arriving immigrants. Dirt and grit, the aviator's bane, will be constantly vacuum-sucked from the great landing and taxiing halls by giant hoses, easily capable of ingesting horses and pianofortes without choking. Why not begin making your own ear plugs, now?

Guided by radio-naphtha waves and therefore needing no motive power of their own, these silent-running five-deck omnibuses will produce enough pure ammonia gas that the profits will underwrite free fares. Monies left over will go to the purchase of Holy Bibles for donation to the expected glut of lunatics.

THE HENRY HUDSON ICEWAY AND THE WEEHAWKEN BRIDGE
GREET R.M.S. ANHEDONIA

See the traffic warden with his speed paddles signalling caution to the Moto-Skates racing north to Yonkers, their riders warmed by hand-held radium stoves. The five-stack liner has just berthed after a 24-hour dash from Southampton on hydro-chemically heated sea lanes, making of the Atlantic a millpond, in time for King Edward VIII to catch the noon Magnetic Train to Niagara Falls to inaugurate the British Empire Elevator Games.

FOR MEN OF HIGH STATION, AN EYRIE
ABOVE THE PIGEONS

With Westchester County and southern Connecticut given over to molyb-denum mining by 1950, wealthy landowners will build stately new homes atop Manhattan's tallest buildings and *parachute* to street level for shopping and the opera. We see in bird's-eye perspective (opposite) a typical Sunday summer's day. Sky-flivvers are winging in to debouch their passengers on the golf links surrounding Nova Moola, a 42-room marvel of prefabricated celluloid in the Moorish-Norman style. But hurry, for the big boxing match is already underway! The giant robots, when not thus entertaining their master's guests, will be found engaged in yard work and rolling carpets. And as they have no brains, they can-not be inflamed and turned against the master by union agitators.

Rocket-powered Newsmobiles like this will speed reporters to and from crime scenes so fast that tomorrow's scoop will be yesterday's news.

COME 1950: WILL YOU BE A "SPEEDIAC" OR A "TRANSIPHOBE"?

So altered will human movement be by 1950 that University experts foresee not only the feebleminded but also normal citizens, thinking they are at a standstill while moving at twenty miles per hour, falling down and breaking their limbs. Why not have your son begin doctor training now?

Present ideas of speed will be transformed. "Autobots" piloted by electric chauffeurs will be too fast to collide. Milady's *billets-doux* will be written in seconds with her self-filling Diesel pen. Baseball-sized *helium balls* will loft messages crosstown from office to office, dethroning King Telegraph.

Life's accelerated pace will dictate new Government strictures. A Kinetic Tax will curb excessive activity with a levy on each individual's "energy index," determined by recording all movement on a knee-mounted meter. Meals will by law be one half-hour in length to lessen the gastric distress of speed eating, enforced by lightning suppertime Board of Health raids on random dwellings. So as not to clog traffic the poor will, for their part, be made to keep moving via dogtrotting "hurry squads" with cudgels.

The New York citizenry of 1950 will divide half and half into Speediacs, shod in dance pumps the faster to move along mirror-smooth city "slidewalks," and Transiphobes, the timid and elderly rooted in the old ways and sullenly resistant to Progress. The latter will be forced out to the suburbs, for New York will be no place for laggards in this new Transportation Age.

NEW YORK'S NEXT 100 YEARS

It's a great, big beautiful tomorrow!

2046

Pitiful to see the old Guggenheim turned into that cheesy rollerskating arena, but in a way it might have all been for the best, because by then it was all wall-to-wall Leroy Niemans anyway. In any event, the arena didn't last long. After that the place sat abandoned for years. Who in his right mind would want to be out and about on that part of Fifth Avenue at nighttime?

Wall Street was now over on Staten Island and the rising tide from global warming promptly flooded most of where it used to be, and there wasn't the money, or the will, to try pushing it back. But those narrow streets, the sharp turns, the squeezed-together buildings, the tricky winds down in that part of town—God, what a lousy boat basin.

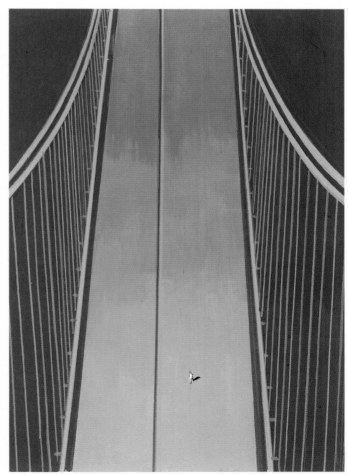

2081

By now enfeebling miasma lay over the city, over everything and everybody in it. Item: The '81 Marathon draws one lone entrant, a homemaker from Iceland. (That's her, in white, just leaving the start line on the Verrazano Narrows Bridge.) She finished 432nd. Okay, an extreme example, but still.

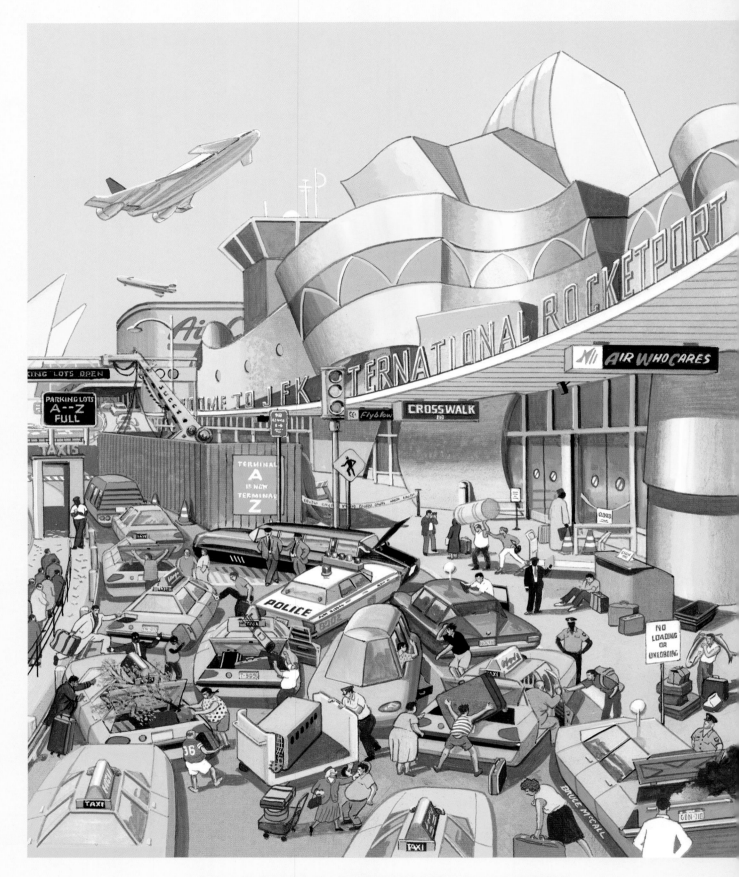

John F. Kennedy Interglobal Rocketport, 2020

BLURB-O-MATIC

An advertisement, circa 1904, for the "Tireless" patented self-perpetuating literary praise machine, capable at peak speed of stamping out as many as one hundred blurbs per minute. Manually operated as it was by a crew of eight blurbists, the Blurb-O-Matic betokened a major forward stride for blurbistry: For the first time, actually reading the book being blurbed was not necessary, and an automatic feature on the random list of famous blurber names ensured that no two blurbs were ever credited to the same person. Technology would later streamline blurbing to uncanny levels of sophistication; by 1938 the process had become so refined that every blurb printed would be cross-referenced with another blurb in the breakthrough "I scratch your back you scratch mine" technique of matching up authors' mutual self-interest.

RAT DREAMS

Recently, Matthew Wilson, a neuroscientist at the Massachusetts Institute of Technology, announced that he had figured out what the rats in his lab dream about. He had implanted tiny electrodes directly into the rats' hippocampi, the region responsible for memory and learning. Then he trained the rats to scurry around a circular track and stop periodically for food rewards. As the rats ran, the electrodes monitored the firing of a dozen or so neurons in each rat's brain. Wilson found that the neurons fired in a distinctive pattern that varied from rat to rat but remained the same for each individual animal.

Later, when the rats experienced rapid eye movement sleep, those neurons began to fire again. Apparently the rats' nocturnal visions are constructed from the mundane events of their daily lives, replayed in detail. Wilson speculates that some rat dreams may be just as convoluted as ours.

That so furtive and repellent a creature as a rat experiences dream states just as we do confirms what many of us have long feared—that rats share far more with us than we want to admit.

762-A, ON DRUGS

Number 762-A was an otherwise archetypal rat with an all-too-familiar case history: born in a slum, abandoned by his parents, existing on scraps, a social misfit forever on the run. Yet 762-A's symptoms fascinated the rat-dream research community. Avoiding the pack, he was a non-joiner, a loner, a recluse. His personal hygiene fell far below even rat standards. Lethargic, no appetite—what ailed 762-A? Three nights of dream tracking yielded dramatic clues. In one dream, 762-A was panicked at finding himself alone in pitch darkness. In another, he was starving but recoiled at the sight of food alive with maggots. And in a dream that induced such stark terror it made his electrodes pop off, 762-A slithered down a sewer pipe and

was confronted by—a mouse. Here was a rodent in despair. Fortunately, the new antidepressant Ratolin has turned the tide. Today 762-A shows every sign of leaving his depression behind. His dreams teem with sexual fantasies, Dumpster orgies, and a scenario in which he races fellow rats up a side of the Empire State Building—and wins.

BROWNIE'S REVENGE

"At first," recalls one mystified researcher, "we thought we'd stuck the electrodes into his hippocampus backward or something." Why were the neuronal patterns traced in the dreams of Brownie, a mature laboratory rat, the virtual opposite of those detected during his waking hours? Then came a stunning revelation: Brownie, a living scientific punching bag, was determined to turn the tables on his keepers. "He was having revenge dreams," a respected

psychorodentologist explains. "In Brownie's secret dreamland, he was a rat in a lab coat forcing hapless humans to perform stupid stunts in the name of science. He was dreaming up some wacky new experiment every night." Thanks to Brownie, a new pathology has been entered into the lexicon of rodent diagnostics: maze rage.

FRANÇOIS'S SENSE OF TASTEFULNESS

Dream research on François, a kitchen rat who lives in a prestigious Parisian seafood restaurant, has shocked rodentologists everywhere by suggesting that genus *Rattus* can decipher human language. Night after night, the messages from François's hippocampus translated into the same dream: eating, eating, eating. But only heaping bowls of ratatouille.

"He could as easily have been dreaming of eating the lobster, the sole, the tender baby octopus," reasons an eminent French analyst. *"Mais non,* only the ratatouille." Could it have been that this denizen of the underworld was responding to a verbal cue? "François hears thousands of words, the garçons ordering scores of different dishes every night," says the analyst, "but he has learned to distinguish words, one from the other. He comes to think, by the sound of the word, that only one dish must be made for him—ratatouille!"

Of course, when actually presented with his first bowl of ratatouille, François sopped up a mouthful and promptly spit it out. Clinical postscript: François has never dreamed of ratatouille since.

EVE'S NIGHTS OF SPLENDOR

The dream life of this female white rat, plucked from her nest in the moth-eaten fire curtain of a decrepit Broadway theater, has yielded an astonishing insight into the question of environment versus heredity. "A rat lives in a dump, eats leftovers, and rarely sees daylight," one therapist observes, "so her typical dream is pretty low-rent. But not this one, not Eve. She dreamed of her cage draped in pink satin, bouquets abounding. In her sleep Eve saw herself as the glamorous queen of the pack, lit always by a brilliant spotlight. Yet there were dark nights when she dreamed of diving headfirst into a bottle, devouring pawfuls of pills."

Eve's dreams are clear evidence that rat behavior is affected by environment. Immersed in a theatrical culture, Eve had absorbed it, identified with it, and in her dream life emulated it. This ordinary rat envisioned herself as no mere skulking, anonymous rodent but as a full-blown Broadway diva.

Rat research is still in its infancy, but researchers are already broadening their scope in search of further insights. Are rat dreams more Jungian than Freudian? Would an eclectic approach make more sense? Can therapy truly make a difference? Will psychopharmacology provide the answer? Balderdash, scoffs the rational human. But will it be the rats that have the last laugh?

Friendlier new IRS offers visitors free coffee.

Forensic comedians close to solving who killed vaudeville.

Havana '52

Unsafe Harbor

Best of all was a balcony suite at one of the casino hotels way up there above Centro Habana, overlooking the harbor and the Malecón seawall. Overlooking just about everything. The horse races across the viaduct—a strange, thrilling, Fellini-esque sight—always began just at sunset in that molten golden light. The free championship boxing matches too—the Chicago Mob staged those and, interestingly enough, made more from the pickpocketing there than from the betting. Such a feel-good place Havana was back then.

Sundays at the Hotel Splendid-Fantastic

The only thing Havana outlawed was boredom, even on Sundays. You saved Sunday morning for the army courts-martial—hardly a dull moment, what with summary judgments and all. Then over to Habana Vieja to stand at a little peephole in a basement while the nuns took their weekly baths. Next came Hotel Splendid–Fantastic for brunch on the terrace and maybe a small wager or two on the aquadivers. Everybody kept saying the diver needed nerves of steel to stand poised up there on the roof waiting, waiting, waiting for the exact right instant to jump so he'd be sure to land smack in that pool of water on top of the biplane put-putting far below. Sure, sure. But what about the bettors? We were waiting, waiting, waiting, too. And it was our money.

Club Alligator

Four thousand nightclubs in Havana and a two-year waiting list for Club Alligator, and it wasn't even a club. It was the Batista regime's maximum-security prison, a dungeon with the sewer system running through, all drip and echo and clammy gloom. Happy *turistas* were free to grab all the champagne and shellfish for Montecristos they wanted as they cruised the twisting stone labyrinth past real live criminals. The air was filled with the sounds of haunting Spanish love songs from the guitars of strolling troubadors headed for the gala lights-out "party" that nobody ever wanted to talk about the next morning—except the cops, who had the photos. Club Alligator was all cash—and lots of it. More, if you declined to hand over your passport. Proceeds, they claimed, went to the Police Benevolent Society. Somebody once cracked wise about there being nothing benevolent about the police in the Batista regime, right in front of a troubador. Poor bastard was never seen again. Poor, dumb, loudmouthed bastard, you might add.

Autopalio

The spirit was just like the Palio in Siena: senseless, nasty ancient blood feuds, all prodded back to life in the form of this breakneck race through Havana's maze of narrow, crooked old backstreets. Only, they used cars instead of horses

and added that very Latin twist of running half the cars clockwise and half counterclockwise. The cops, who ran their own Policía entry, always made sure a few lug nuts were loose or sugar got into the fuel tanks. It was an insanely macho thing, dozens of expensive cars careening around and around, bouncing off walls, pedals to the metal, kids tossing bottles off balconies and strewing the streets with nails. Suicidal, you might sneer. But no; that was the energy of the old Havana breaking through, the life force of a passionate people, and if not for outlets like the Autopalio, there would have been a revolution long before.

ABOUT THE AUTHOR

Beginning with his work for the *National Lampoon* in the early Seventies, Bruce McCall has published a prolific flow of parodic, satirical, and surreal humor, both written and illustrated, in almost every major publication in the United States and Canada. He has been a frequent contributor to *The New Yorker* since 1980, and his work regularly appears in *Vanity Fair* and the *New York Times*. His 1982 humor collection, *Zany Afternoons*, has become a collectors' item, and 1999 show of his paintings at New York's James Goodman Gallery almost sold out. The Canadian-born McCall pursued careers in commercial art, automotive journalism, and advertising before yielding to a lifelong impulse and becoming a full-time humor freelancer in 1993. His critically acclaimed memoir of growing up Canadian, *Thin Ice,* was published in 1997 and was made into a documentary by the National Film Board of Canada. In 2001, he published *The Last Dream-o-Rama,* a tongue-in-cheek history of Detroit's dream car era. Bruce McCall lives in New York City and is still a Canadian citizen.